FIT to SHOW

FIT to SHOW
The Guide to Grooming Your Horse

Frank Madden

and

Bill Cooney

with

Amy Rosi

Photographs by James Parker

ARCO PUBLISHING, INC.
New York

Facing title page: Meg Sullivan and Kenmere Farm's Lion in Winter.

On the cover: Playing Games, owned by Mr. and Mrs. Paul Newman and daughter Clea of Westport, Connecticut. A consistent champion at all the major shows, including the National Horse Show at Madison Square Garden where he won the Large Junior Hunter championship for two consecutive years. Ridden here by Jenno Topping, winner of the 1984 USET East Coast finals, with the horse's groom, Peggy Hedman.

Published by Arco Publishing, Inc.
215 Park Avenue South, New York, N.Y. 10003

Copyright © 1985 by Frank Madden and Bill Cooney

Library of Congress Cataloging-in-Publication Data

Madden, Frank.
  Fit to show.

  Includes index.
  1. Horses—Grooming. 2. Horses—Showing.
I. Cooney, Bill. II. Rosi, Amy. III. Title.
SF285.7.M33 1985   636.1'0833   85-13419
ISBN 0-668-06444-7

Printed in the United States of America

10 9 8 7 6 5 4 3 2 1

The following products mentioned in this book are Registered in the U.S. Patent
and Trademark Office: Corona, No More Tangles, Vaseline, Ace Bandage, Weladol, Vetrolin, Lexol, Properts, Ivory, Pinesol, DeFungit, Fiebing's Hoof Dressing, Blue-Kote, Panalog, Azium, Uptite, Listerine, Lady Clairol, Duraglit, Betadine, Bon Ami Cleanser, Comet, A & D Ointment, Kendall, Quick Silver,
Captan, Omolene, Velcro, and Vetrap.

Kopertox is a trademark of Frankling Lab, Inc.

To all the horses and people who have
given us the knowledge over the years
to make the writing of this book
possible. We want to thank you all,
and will remember you always.

Contents

Tables

Foreword

Over the past forty years I've watched the sport of hunter-jumper equitation showing grow and grow. It seems incredible to think back to those early years after World War II. Many of the shows we hacked to. They were often one-day shows and gasoline was still rationed. In those days many of us kept horses and ponies at home as well as at the nearby riding clubs or professional barns. We learned to take care of our animals ourselves. While the care was simple and basic, it helped us develop a feel for an animal and to become all-around horsemen. When going to a smaller show we often did almost everything ourselves. Occasionally I'd coax my mother into holding my horse—either for tacking-up purposes or for grazing. She was terrified! Nonetheless, horse shows in those days, while as fiercely competitive as they are today, were more of a family outing, had a more leisurely time frame, and were much more relaxed. A lunch break and exhibitors' parties later in the afternoon were the rule for the day rather than the exception. Twelve braids in a mane were more likely than thirty and a riding coat would do, not tailored *haute couture*. Our horses were "broke"—barely—and as a rule bent to the outside, not the inside, of the ring.

Along with the tremendous leap forward in riding, training, and teaching has come an incredible advance in stable management, shoeing, and veterinary science. In fact, each aspect of riding and showing now has its specialists. Riders are sophisticated technicians today, many of them capable of winning over an Olympic course. The teachers and trainers are aware of every possible exercise and tactic to further their protégés, whether horses or riders. Vets today could operate the Mayo Clinic, and blacksmiths have a correction for every possible problem under any and all conditions. Perhaps, though, the greatest specialist (and I'd dare say artist) in his trade is the experienced groom. The time, effort, and knowledge it takes today to get a horse to the ring is truly mind-boggling. It is simple maintenance, yes. To do a first-class job, though, requires detail, and that is what this book is all about.

Frank Madden and Bill Cooney, longtime associates of mine, have provided us all with a very important book. It is important not only for the people who work in barn areas but also (and especially) for riders and teachers who find themselves away from the stable. While many young horsemen have advanced their riding, teaching, and training abilities, their growth is stunted when it comes to stable management and all that this encompasses. Believe it or not, these young professionals sometimes do not really know much about horses, conformation, soundness, maintenance, and ailments. And the more proficient they become away from the barn, the less they relate, in the true sense of the word, to the horse. This is a real crime, and it can be seen to affect the horse business from top to bottom today. The good all-around horseman, the one who truly knows horses, is a dying breed. Only the limited specialist, good as he or she may be, is here to replace him. That is not good enough. We must all try to broaden our base and learn about other areas of horsemanship.

Nothing in this book is particularly new. Rather, the material covered is basic, simple, and traditional. The important thing is that the details of every technique are covered and explained in a step-by-step sequence. It is a "how-to" book in the best sense of the word. Anyone can read it and understand it right away, and that is most basic to education—simplicity. Good stable management revolves around these things: safety, humanity, and cleanliness. These points are emphasized over and over in this book. Read *Fit to Show* and you will be well on your way toward understanding how to properly run a first-class riding establishment and, perhaps, if you're lucky, becoming a horseman in the true sense of the word.

GEORGE H. MORRIS

Pittstown, New Jersey

Introduction

What does it mean—fit to show? To Frank Madden and Bill Cooney, two of the nation's top hunter/jumper trainers, it means a horse that is carefully tended both physically and mentally. When one of their horses comes through the in-gate, it is groomed to win—turned out with meticulous attention to detail. There is no quick way to ready a horse for the show ring, "no shortcuts," as Frank Madden says again and again to the riders and grooms at Beacon Hill. "Whatever is worth doing is worth doing well," reiterates Bill Cooney, who is known for his demanding standards at the barn and in the show ring.

Madden and Cooney operate a hunter/jumper show barn called Beacon Hill, in North Salem, New York. In the last few years, the pair has guided many notable junior riders to the nation's top equestrian awards—the coveted AHSA and ASPCA Maclay medals, the USET finals, and numerous junior hunter and jumper championships on the prestigious A-rated horse show circuit. In 1984, the team made horse show history by being the first trainers to guide their juniors to the "triple crown" of horsemanship awards, winning the USET finals and the AHSA and Maclay medals in a single year. Their student Francesca Mazella, at fifteen years of age, became the first junior rider to win both the Medal and Maclay in eighteen years, and seventeen-year-old Jenno Topping won the fiercely competitive USET finals at the United States Equestrian Team headquarters in Gladstone, New Jersey.

Fitting a horse to show could really be considered a working art form. A horse in motion in the hunter ring takes its inspiration from the hunt field—competition steeped in tradition and ritual, yet created to challenge a horse and rider in search of victory over obstacles.

At Beacon Hill there is definitely only one way to turn out a horse for the hunter/jumper rings. The style has been established by precedents born out of functional needs. For example, a horse's mane was originally braided for the hunt field to keep it from flying and getting caught up in the whip and reins. Today, braiding not only serves this purpose, but

Jenno Topping of Sagaponack, New York, with former USET coach Bert DeNemethy, accepting the award for winning the 1984 USET East Coast finals at the United States Equestrian Headquarters in Gladstone, New Jersey. By winning the USET finals, Ms. Topping secured the first leg of the triple crown of the 1984 horsemanship awards for trainers Bill Cooney and Frank Madden.

shows off the long, elegant neck of the thoroughbred horse—so favored in this country—and makes him more attractive to the eye.

"Don't forget we are at a horse show," says Bill, ever the stylist. "We want our horses to look as good as they can."

Nothing, perhaps, is as awe inspiring as a brace of Beacon Hill horses, groom on hand, lined up at the in-gate with their beautifully aligned braids, flawlessly clean and shiny coats and legs, painted and glistening hooves, and shimmering tails with their decorative braids. The riders sit poised, perfectly matched to their mounts, eyes riveted on Bill and Frank for last-minute directions and encouragement.

The grooms, farriers, braiders, and veterinarians who work behind the scenes at Beacon Hill to produce these finely turned out animals are horsemen first, as are Bill Cooney and Frank Madden. *Horseman* is the operative word, and it means treating an animal not only correctly, but excellently, allowing the horse to do and look his very best in the show ring. "The ring is not the place to do your homework" is one of Bill Cooney's favorite admonitions to new riders and grooms. A painstakingly slow, day-to-day routine is followed, and once Beacon Hill is at a show, the staff simply put into high gear a system they practice every day. There are no serious problems, no corrections or camouflage. The horses look immaculate and act superbly and are regarded with respect by both officials and their fiercest competitors. As one ASHA judge observed, "I could have looked at one particular Beacon Hill horse all day. It was simply a pleasure to watch him. His appearance attracted me."

Bill Cooney gives last-minute in-gate instructions to an intent Arianne deKwiatkowski at the USET East Coast finals, September 1984.

What does it take to have this winning edge? If you look through this book for secrets, tricks of the trade, or magic formulas you may be disappointed. Beacon Hill's method is surprisingly simple. What it takes is incredibly hard work and strict attention to detail. "Keep it simple" is one of Frank Madden's favorite phrases, and "We are traditionalists" is the way Bill Cooney sums up their endeavor. They are more than eager to share their expertise and knowledge. They themselves learned from the ground up, over the years, by putting themselves in a position to learn from the best, and—even today—by turning to the experts when they need help. They invite all horse lovers and horsemen to share in their particular method of turning out a horse to their satisfaction. It is a system that can work for all horses and all horsemen.

There are hundreds of useful tips in this book that should help you whether you show hunters or Western pleasure horses. With the exception of braiding and certain tack appointments, which are specifically for hunters, this grooming guide is designed to make every horse "fit to show." Good animal husbandry and grooming relate to every type of horse and riding discipline. Any talented horse should look like a winner, as well as perform like one.

1

Grooming in Perspective

Beacon Hill horses are basically winners to start
with. The management is in the care and training.
These horses are maneuvered, not manufactured.

Marion Hulick
horse management consultant

Our method of turning out an ideal hunter or jumper really has two
objectives: to make sure he peaks when he should through good grooming
and training, and to keep him in show condition as he endures the long,
arduous season that uses up nine months of his life every year.

One of the best things you can do for your horse is to give him the rest
and contentment he needs to relieve stress. We try to teach our students
and grooms to learn to sense how a horse is feeling. One of the first
questions we ask after a rider has been in the schooling ring is, "How's he
feel?" Riders have to develop a reaction to their horses. Our goal is for our
riders to become horsemen, and a horseman senses how his horse is feeling. He can anticipate a problem, or learn to make the most of a strength.
You can tell a lot just by a horse's expression.

Grooms are invaluable in this area. Even the most subtle change is felt
by a sensitive groom. They rub those horses' bodies and finger those
tendons so often they can discover the most infinitesimal flaws or swellings—and can literally save a situation. Their chief role is to prevent
problems from happening, through maintenance and observation. This
should be any horseman's objective, and one even a single horse owner can
practice. Get to know your horse intimately. Watch for changes in his
body or attitude. Remember, you are striving to produce a horse that is
both mentally and physically sound.

This is a good place to acquaint you with our rigorous show schedule,
so that you can better understand what is expected of our riders and
horses, and how great a task it is to keep them both really "fit to show."

1

The hunter/jumper show year divides itself naturally into four segments, each with its own demands and objectives. It begins right after the National Horse Show, which is always held during the first week in November at Madison Square Garden in New York City. The National Horse Show is the most prestigious show of the year for us, and it ends with the Maclay finals on Sunday. On Monday, without a day in between to rest up, we begin our new year. This is the time new riders and horses are taken on, new partnerships formed. Juniors who have reached their eighteenth birthday will be graduating from the junior ranks, and moving on to the higher grades of riding. Some may need a new horse, which we'll help them find, to compete in the amateur/owner and jumper divisions. New goals must be established for the riders commencing another show year. December is a time of rest and a time to re-evaluate. It is also a time to go to work recuperating and relaxing, making the new horses we purchased, or the ones we have "let down," fit to show again.

From December through April, we move our entire operation down to Florida for the winter show circuit. Our main concern at this time is with making the horses fit enough to ship and adjust to the transition in climate. Once settled in Florida, we have to work to bring them back to total show fitness, after their months of rest coupled with light work in November and December. While we are based in Florida, our riders commute from schools and residences throughout the country to show their horses. We return to New York in mid April for what we call the second swing, which includes the Children's Services Show in Farmington, Connecticut, and the famous Devon Horse Show in Pennsylvania, held in May.

The grueling third quarter of the year is organized to allow those riders already qualified for the AHSA Medal and Maclay to expand and grow by showing at selected shows in the hunter, jumper, and equitation divisions. For those not yet qualified, this part of the year involves a strategic show schedule involving the necessary AHSA Medal, Maclay, or USET classes. All this ends by Labor Day, and sometime in mid September fall the USET finals at the United States Equestrian Team training facility in Gladstone, New Jersey.

The final wind-down is the culmination of our year—the prestigious fall indoor shows: the Pennsylvania National Horse Show (AHSA Medal finals) in Harrisburg, the Washington International, and the National Horse Show.

The preceding summary gives you some idea of our schedule. Through this time, our main objective is to try to make the horses look and feel at the end of those nine months exactly like they did at the beginning—or as close to it as possible. The way to ensure this is with a careful work and feeding plan, and with a daily regime strictly followed by grooms and riders to provide continuity in the horses' care. That's what

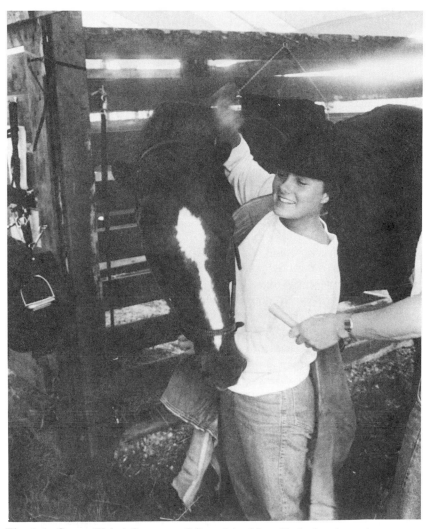

Fig. 1-1. Owner Kristi Gertsner of Scarsdale, New York, laughs as her groom offers her jumper The Artesian the first of many carrots that day. Carrots help make winners, because Artie won the Junior Jumper class that day and helped make Kristi Leading Junior Rider at the 1984 International Show Jumping Derby in Portsmouth, Rhode Island.

we really mean by putting grooming in perspective. In addition to being the right and humane way to care for a horse, good grooming is the key to maintaining and maneuvering these great athletes , as consultant Marion Hulick so aptly puts it. A show horse must always appear to look his very best effortlessly.

Selecting the Best Raw Materials

Packaging a horse and rider combination is the number one priority in the hunter world and in hunt seat equitation. It is the total picture—horse and rider. Although it is the rider who is being judged in an equitation class, that magic combination of suitable horse to suitable rider is what makes for a sound performance with style.

If you are aiming to have the best-looking finished product in the show ring, or even in your own backyard, you should try to start with the best raw material you can find. And you should think about suitability. When we search out a new hunter, jumper, or equitation horse for one of our customers, we take into account the proportion of horse to rider so that the total picture will be pleasing to the eye. We are striving for a total impression—a freeze-frame in a judge's mind. We feel that the proportion and appearance of the horse and rider, coupled with depth of ability, are what make the winning edge.

This is one aspect to consider when selecting a new horse, and it is something over which you have a degree of control. Obviously, a rider with short legs should not consider a horse with a large barrel. A small rider can look very satisfactory on a tall horse if the barrel is narrow and the sides sloping. Conversely, a tall, slender girl needs an elongated, elegant horse. One of our riders is tall and slender, and her horse is similar in stature. Since you are working on the picture of horse and rider together, a horse may be acceptable even if he is not showy and doesn't have perfect conformation. Another of our students showed a solid-colored, strong, big-boned horse with real ring presence but no special markings or attractiveness. In this case, the rider's ability, in a sense, added the white legs the horse wasn't lucky enough to be born with. Rider influence has as much to do with suitability as conformation and a complement of horse and rider proportions. It helps, however, to start with a pleasing picture. And don't ignore the asset of coloring. A blond rider looks especially stunning on a chestnut. A dark-haired rider looks elegant on a black horse. If possible, try to consider these details of height, frame, and color when choosing a show horse.

We like our hunter and equitation horses to have a bloom, to be slightly rounded. This can come only from a regimented feeding and grooming program combined with proper exercise. Weight put on a horse in a short period of time by overfeeding without exercise may very well melt away as soon as the animal is put back into work. Not only that, but it will be fat and not rounded muscle—the athletic ideal. Feeding for fitness is in itself a topic, which we cover in Chapter 2.

Although this is not a training book, but basically a book about grooming and horse care, it is sometimes difficult to separate the two, they are so intertwined. Certain forms of good animal husbandry border on training aids. A horse that is conditioned, with good skin and muscle tone due to proper care and good food, can do more with less stress and stay healthy longer.

Although we have devised a system that works well for us and turns our horses out to our satisfaction, you will find some contradictions in the text that follows. The explanation is that every horse must be treated as an individual, and you have to employ those remedies that will work best in a given situation. While we do insist that our grooms and staff adhere to our system of horse care and grooming, we are always open to advances and different ways to handle a problem. There isn't a day that goes by in which a horseman doesn't learn something new, and we are constantly learning from the excellent horsemen who surround us in our work.

Health First

Before you begin to work the devastatingly long hours it takes to ready a horse to show, you should be certain your horse is healthy. Any new horse at our barn is given a thorough going-over by our attending veterinarian. And the grooms will check him from head to toe as well. We make sure he has been wormed and has his proper flu, tetanus, and rhino (rhinopneumonitis) vaccines. If there is any doubt about his soundness we will have him x-rayed. In fact, we x-ray our show horses two times a year, at the conclusion of the fall indoor shows and in the spring when we return from Florida, just to alert us to any changes in bone mass. A Coggins test for equine infectious anemia is required in most states, but we may also do a blood test to determine whether a horse has any vitamin deficiencies or anemia if his mental or physical attitude suggests this.

In a show barn, herd health is an adjunct to good animal husbandry and grooming. For instance, you can't imagine how quickly a case of fungus can spread through a barn if a new horse arrives with one and his brushes or blankets are used on other horses. And worms can be spread through improper control of flies and removal of manure in the barn and turnout area. Both fungus and worms can ruin a horse's coat. A fungus will cause sores and raw patches to appear where the hair has fallen out, while a load of intestinal worms can make a horse's coat dull and shaggy.

We worm our horses every two months. Before the appearance of worming medications that kill all parasite worms in a single dose, we would alternate medications and methods, i.e., tubing, paste, and as top dressings in feed. We continue to do this because horses become resistant to the same products used repeatedly. Even though today's new wormers seem to be 100 percent effective, and the horses are not supposed to become resistant to them, we still think it is a good idea to alternate methods and the products used.

To kill fungus and bacteria, we disinfect stalls and buckets on a regular basis. Bedding is changed weekly, and supplemented as needed. At the first signs of fungus on a horse we use topical mixtures sponged or sprayed on the affected areas, and add fungicides to bath water, as well as disinfecting all grooming brushes, tools, saddle pads, and other materials the horse has come in contact with.

Because our horses travel constantly and are exposed to numerous viruses and other infectious conditions, we routinely have them vaccinated twice a year, in the spring and fall. They are given a "four-in-one shot," which protects them from tetanus toxin, Eastern and Western encephalo-myelitis, and flu, and a separate vaccine for rhino.

We make sure that the barn is well ventilated, and have an automatic fly control system that pumps out a spray every forty-five minutes. We insist on an immaculate barn—aisleways and stalls are dusted daily to rid them of dust and cobwebs. This is not just for the sake of appearance. Dust, mold, and other forms of barn dirt are unhealthy to both horses and people. They create a bacterial environment and are hard on lungs, coats, eyes, and feet.

Another important safeguard to ensure a healthy horse is a systematic program of expert care—regularly scheduled visits by vets, farriers, dentists, and others. Our vet observes our horses on a weekly basis, our farrier checks our horses at least every three or four weeks, and we arrange for our dentist to float our horses' teeth at least once a year.

2

Feeding for Fitness

A horse's weight and temperament will never lie
to you.

General Principles

The first thing we do to a new horse at Beacon Hill after he's been
examined by our veterinarian is check and correct his weight. (We might
say that for riders as well! As we said, we like our hunters rounded, but we
like our riders thin and fit, like athletes.) We keep our horses fatter than
many barns do and some trainers fault us for this, but we like the look. It
is a science to keep horses rounded, and fit both mentally and physically.
Grooms and riders new to our regime are amazed that we want them as
rounded as we do. "He'll get fat," we'll hear a rider say when a groom
sneaks her charge another carrot during the day.

Objectives

We in the horse show business are trying to find a balanced diet for
each individual horse, one that produces the appearance we desire and the
fitness each needs to get the job done in the ring. You can actually make a
horse too fit for the task he is called upon to perform. For example, what is
required to feed a hunter is very different from what is required to keep a
jumper in shape and strong. For a hunter you want a horse that looks
rounded, with superb muscle tone, but with a relaxed, not overly ener-
getic mental attitude. You should strive in your feeding and conditioning
for anaerobic fitness—fitness of the soft tissues. A jumper, however, needs
enormous reserves of energy and nerve and incredible heart and lung
capacity—aerobic fitness. As everyone today knows, this involves stimu-

7

lating cardiovascular function through the intake of air. Controlling fitness is the natural way to control a horse's mental and physical attitude.

Food, Energy, and Attitude

The subject of food, energy, and attitude is a sophisticated one. Food can make a horse happy, or it can depress him—you can see the results of too little or too much grain in as little as two weeks. The amount of food a horse on the show circuit receives daily can depend on how he is performing on any given day, and is not necessarily determined on a routine basis. Was the horse nervous? Did he seem tense? Did he have too much energy—or not enough strength? A hunter needs to be relaxed in the ring, and you can actually suppress excess energy by cutting back on grain rations. This slight cutback, when coupled with exercise, acts as a natural depressant because you are not replenishing the energy-building protein the horse is using up in the show ring. On the other hand, you can build a horse up by increasing his feed—not by changing his body weight and appearance, but by increasing his energy intake. A jumper, for instance, might receive a small grain ration with a high protein level (say, 16 percent). This would give him the strength to perform while still keeping him thin and not overexcited.

Horses are similar to human beings in that some utilize feed and conditioning better than others because they are more efficient metabolically. The secret of feeding for fitness is ending up with a horse carrying legitimate weight—weight that will turn to muscle in the body.

Feeding

Basic Feed

We feed our horses twice a day at the same times each day or as close to them as possible—ideally 7 A.M. and 5 P.M. Feeding the correct amount, on time, does as much to keep a horse healthy and happy as anything else in our regime.

Both hunters and jumpers need foods high in carbohydrates, but not fat-producing. An all-purpose pellet feed, and hay, will provide the proper amount. We feed a combination of pellets mixed with sweet feed (for weight and palatability) that contains about 12 percent protein. The amount of feed for each horse is typically eight quarts a day, but this varies according to the individual horse. (This is a good average amount for a pleasure horse as well.) Jumpers may get considerably more and be fed a

Fig. 2-1. Assistant barn manager Evan Davidson steers the feed wheelbarrow down the barn aisle—adhering to a strict schedule. At Beacon Hill, we feed an all-purpose pellet mixed with a smaller ratio of sweet feed. While grain rations may vary, tailored to a horse's individual needs, we rarely use top dressings or supplements.

grain with a higher protein level and less carbohydrate, such as whole or crimped oats. With today's advanced commercial feeds, more and more barns are relying on a combination of pellets and sweet feed for high levels of energy and less fat instead of turning to whole oats, or the more digestible crimped oats, as the racehorse industry has always done, as oats can make a horse too hot.

Hay is high in carbohydrates, and we feed it freely, keeping it in front of our horses at all times unless they have a weight problem. Many people are surprised by the amount of hay we give, but we use it as a time consumer as well as a nutrient. We are dealing with show horses who must remain in their stalls for long periods of time when they're on the circuit, and the hay gives them something to do. We feed a timothy hay or a timothy/alfalfa mix, not pure alfalfa, which is too rich and can cause digestive problems such as colic and diarrhea. We encounter many types of hay on the road, and we always reach for the less rich.

Vitamins and Supplements

Many people are surprised that a show barn such as ours doesn't rely on special non-commercial feed mixtures for each individual horse and top dressings and supplements to add vitamins and bloom. But in a barn where you are feeding large numbers of horses at one time this is not always practical or necessary. We do make sure our horses get salt licks in their stalls. We also feed them electrolytes in their grain or water as a precaution. Electrolytes are trace minerals that can be lost through sweat and work, especially in hot weather, and must be replaced as a horse with an electrolyte deficiency can become severely dehydrated (see *Dehydration*, pages 11–12).

Because of our health and feeding program, we rarely encounter a horse suffering from a vitamin or mineral deficiency but if his appearance or attitude indicates that there is one we simply ask the vet to take a blood sample and rely on his suggestions as to what commercial tonic or supplement to use. One vitamin deficiency that is often found in some show barns, where the horses are not able to be turned out, is a lack of vitamins A and D, which are absorbed through sunlight. These vitamins affect hair and skin, so they are an essential grooming aid. It is important for horses to get a source of light, and turning them out daily is the best way to get a supply of vitamins A and D.

Some people recommend putting oil in the grain ration to help produce a shiny coat. You may have noticed that when the vet doses a colicky horse with mineral oil, about two days later his coat really blooms and shines. This is because of the oil. But we are talking about gallons—an enormous quantity for a pound-per-pound effect. A tablespoon a day, which is what is usually suggested, really has little or no effect, in our opinion, except perhaps on a cumulative basis if you add it religiously over a long period of time. You don't produce shiny coats with oil or top dressings in the feed—you do it with elbow grease!

Bran Mashes

Stables are traditionally closed on Monday, and because Monday is a day of rest, and usually follows a weekend of showing, this seems the ideal day to offer a bran mash to the horses. A bran mash helps to purge a horse's digestive system, which is not the most efficient in the animal kingdom. A bran mash is also often an excellent natural remedy for relaxing a horse after he's had colic, or any other time you want to soothe his system, such as after the disruptive effects of long-distance vanning. We give a bran mash for two consecutive feedings before we ship long distances. It's also a nice offering for a show horse on a cold night—like a hot toddy for a cold horseman. The recipe that follows is a simple, modern one, easier to fix than the traditional cooked mash produced in large vats.

Modern-Day Bran Mash Recipe

Mix 2 quarts bran mash with 1½ quarts sweet feed.

Moisten with just enough warm water to make it fluffy but still maintain a consistency that will be palatable to a horse (not like oatmeal).

Carrots, apples, and molasses may be added as a treat. Use about ½ cup molasses, but be aware that this gets rather messy.

Special Problems

Dehydration

Show horses can easily suffer from dehydration because of the loss of salt and trace minerals (electrolytes) through working and sweating. Poor water drinkers also get easily dehydrated. Dehydration can cause weight loss and make a horse appear gaunt. A simple way to determine if a horse is dehydrated is to pinch his neck by grabbing a fold of skin. The skin should slip immediately back to the neck. If the horse is dehydrated, the skin fold will remain stuck together for a while. Dehydration can be countered by adding electrolytes to water or grain rations (if your horse is a poor drinker) and by making sure your horse is drinking his water.

The Underweight Horse

It is easy to make a horse fat. But that is merely the tip of the iceberg. You have to determine why he is underweight for long-range success. The first thing we do is check out a horse's physical and mental attitude. If he is thin because he needs worming and/or more grain, or because he has some deficiency (vitamins B, A, and D, iron, and enzyme are all common), a blood test, worming, and observation, plus a few weeks of extra grain, will do wonders for him. If he is thin because he is nervous—either in work or in his stall—we try to correct this condition.

A lot of horses can worry themselves thin. A horse will not eat in a stressful situation. Check out your horse's stall. Is there too much commotion? Is he nervous in his stall? Is it clean—the buckets washed, and uneaten loose hay removed instead of piled up in a corner to turn rancid underneath? A horse will not drink from a dirty bucket or eat happily in an unkempt stall.

Another key to making a horse fat is to increase his appetite. He has to want to eat. There are several ways to do this. One is to be sure he is getting enough exercise to make him hungry. This will help develop a healthy appetite. You can also increase his expectation about eating by always feeding him slightly less than he wants. Leave him a little hungry and anticipating his next meal. Make sure he runs out of hay. This coupled with proper exercise will make a horse a better eater.

One way to help increase weight on a fussy eater is to keep a hay net with fresh hay in front of him at all times. The hay won't get pawed or wet and rancid in a hay net. When you hang a net, make sure it is hung at the horse's shoulder level so he can't get his feet caught in it.

If overwork or stress while working are the causes of a show horse's weight problem, the first thing you have to do is find a point in his schedule when you can take the time to dramatically change his eating habits and appearance. You will need at least three weeks. The ideal time in our show schedule is during the months of November and December, when the horses are not showing. It is much harder to add weight to a horse while you are still coping with the problem that is causing it. Sometimes you are not fortunate enough to find a break in the show schedule and keeping weight on becomes a constant battle under show pressure.

Then you have to resort to consistent feeding schedules with plenty of hay and grain to offset the effects of energy expended and nerves frayed.

If you do get a break, you should try to build up weight by gradually increasing the horse's grain ration while allowing him to conserve his energy by giving him stall rest and only light exercise. According to the veterinarians we have consulted, you can safely increase a horse's feed ration by up to two quarts a feeding without harmful effects. You may need to take a week or more to increase the amount of grain significantly enough to achieve the results you are after. In an extreme case, an underweight horse may get as much as sixteen quarts a day (eight quarts a feeding) for a short period of time.

Be careful not to increase the grain ration too quickly or you may bring on a case of founder or colic. Early signs of founder (laminitis) are stiffness or tenderness in stance, and accelerated pulse or heat in the foot coupled very often with fever and acute pain. The horse is by nature a grazing animal and not constituted to digest grain. Rapid increase in grain consumption produces harmful buildups of histamines and toxins in the system, which cause swelling in the laminae in the hoof, leading in extreme cases to rotation of the bone in the foot. A horse that has ingested too much grain for his system, or who has eaten an unfamiliar grain, may also develop colic. Colic is acute indigestion. It causes severe abdominal pain and can be fatal, which is why we are extra careful about grain rations. In either instance, if symptoms appear, especially if you know there has been a change in a horse's schedule, consult a veterinarian.

One other thing to watch out for when you are trying to put weight on a horse by increasing his grain ration while conserving him physically is tying up. This is a severe case of muscle cramps that can lead to temporary paralysis if not treated properly. It is a result of amino acids storing up and settling in the horse's kidneys because the protein in his system is not being sufficiently used up in work. If your horse starts to get tight and cramped behind or his muscles are trembling after a workout or cold bath, he could well be tying up—again, consult your vet immediately.

The Overweight Horse

Being overweight is as unhealthy for a horse as being underweight, although we feel that a hunter looks shapelier in the ring if he's more rounded and heavier than is the ideal for other performance horses.

As with the underweight horse, the first thing you have to determine before you put your horse on a diet is why he is overweight. If he is in work and fit but overweight, then you must reduce food intake and lower the amount of fat-producing carbohydrates in his feed. If he is fat and soft

TABLE 2.1
FEEDING FOR FITNESS

Maintenance: Decide what grain and hay ration works for your horse's work and show schedule. (Most hunters need an average of 8 quarts a day.) Feed all-purpose pellets mixed with sweet feed. Feed at the same times every day. Worm every 2 to 3 months and float teeth annually. Provide salt licks and, in warm weather, electrolytes in water or grain ration. Wash buckets daily and remove uneaten hay.

Underweight horse: Determine cause—mental attitude or physical problem. Worm, float teeth, and increase grain and hay rations slowly. Try to find a break in showing schedule and keep exercise to minimum. May take 2 or 3 months to attain desired weight.

Overweight horse: Decide whether horse is fit and overweight, or fat and soft from too much food and too little work. Decrease feed rations, especially hay, which are high in fat-producing carbohydrates. Check mental attitude. If the horse is out of shape, reduce weight and food as you increase exercise to avoid creating heavy, muscle-bound horse.

Showing: Horses traveling the show circuit need to eat the same type of grain consistently. Change of feed can cause hives or colic and make a horse go off his feed. Transport your grain with you to shows.

Purge system: Feed bran mash after colic attack, before shipping long distances, or anytime the horse's system is disrupted to help avoid blockage and colic.

Young horse (under four years): Regardless of work schedule or mental attitude, 8 to 12 quarts of feed a day are needed in order to get the right amount of nutrients, vitamins, and minerals for growth. But be careful not to overfeed, as this can lead to health problems and unsoundness.

Older horse: The older horse needs grain he can chew and digest with his longer teeth and uneven grinding surface. An average of 8 to 12 quarts of all-purpose pellets is probably best. He may need supplements. Have teeth floated and keep up with worming program.

Dehydration: Add powdered electrolytes to grain or water ration in warm weather. Provide salt lick.

Shipping: Before traveling long distances, give bran mash for two consecutive feedings. The day before, have horse tubed with oil by vet to avoid blockage. Stop and offer horse water every 4 hours. Feed half normal ration during shipping. Try to arrange for stopover if trip is over 12 hours.

because he has been overfed and let down, once you put him back in work the weight will begin to melt away. A word of caution, however: If you take a horse who is out of shape and overweight and start him back immediately on a conditioning program to build up his muscles and endurance, you will actually turn some of that excess fat into hard muscle. Then you will have an animal who is fit but still outsized. Show horses with this appearance look exaggerated.

Muscle is harder to reduce than fat, so it is important to get your horse to the proper weight before you start to increase exercise. Excess weight is also a danger to a performance horse's structural soundness and can cause anemia and chemical deficiencies, which affect physical condition and mental attitude.

To reduce a horse's weight his food intake will need to be cut back at a rate of two quarts of grain a feeding over a week or so, plus a reduction of his hay ration. We have horses in our barn getting only two quarts of grain and hay and maintaining their ideal weight. They metabolize their food better than some other horses. Horsemen will sometimes say that a horse can "live on air." Don't feel that there is a certain amount you must feed your horse. You have to do some experimenting and evaluation. You might consider selecting a high-energy grain such as whole or crimped oats, or feeding pellets without adding rich sweet feed.

Teeth

The grinding surface of a horse's teeth is what pulverizes his grain and helps make it digestible. Without dental aid, the teeth continue to grow and can actually become so uneven and hooked that the horse loses most of his grinding surface. When this happens, you will find whole grain around the feeder or floor. Older horses need more dental attention than younger ones because their teeth are longer and digestion becomes more difficult as they age. Uneven teeth may also actually bypass a horse's bite and cause pain when he is wearing a bit or cuts inside his mouth.

We have our horses' teeth floated at least once a year by a professional horse dentist, and any horse that comes to our barn looking undernourished has his teeth checked to see if he needs floating. What horse dentists do is file hooked teeth down to a flatter grinding surface and a good one can actually realign teeth to help a horse accept the bit better if he has a problem. A veterinarian can also float a horse's teeth.

3

Conditioning

Always think in terms of time when you think of
conditioning.

One of the primary ways to get a horse in shape, or back in shape, is a
carefully plotted schedule of exercise, food, and good grooming. There is
no substitute for the rub rag and hours of daily grooming, and the same
can be said of conditioning programs. There are no shortcuts. You have to
decide upon a system that is worked out to fulfill your horse's needs. We
post a seven-day work sheet, filled in daily, that alerts our grooms and
riders to the exercise/conditioning program we have selected for their
horses. We always alter the weekly routines to encompass different forms
of conditioning—for example, in a given week they might include flat
work, trail rides, turnout, longeing, and lessons, in addition to the showing schedule. Grooms and riders are trained to think of all these regimes in
terms of time, and not just of the type of exercise—the time needed at
each activity, or each gait, to achieve the desired result without straining
the horse. It might be a forty-minute lesson, a half-hour trail ride, a
twenty-minute longeing session. You must always be alert to fatigue. You
do not want to work your horse to the point of exhaustion, but to gradually
build up his endurance and muscle stamina.

As we've said, you can make your horse too fit for the job you are
training him to perform. Before you begin a conditioning program, figure
out what the performance demands on your horse are going to be. Do you
want him anaerobically (soft tissue) or aerobically (heart and lung) fit? A
hunter needs to combine both, and a jumper needs to be more aerobically
fit. It is possible to give a horse too much stamina and energy, so that
you're riding too much animal and can't even touch bottom in the show
ring.

Some horses stay fitter than others, just as some people do. These
horses seem to get the most out of whatever exercise they are doing, while
others become soft more quickly and need more conditioning.

17

There are many effective ways to condition a horse. Each one has a particular advantage, either for the horse, or because it suits the needs of a rider or trainer based on his facilities and availability. Anytime a horse is in motion and using his body—either moving free or in a controlled situation—he is being conditioned. Among the different forms of conditioning are long walks under saddle, trail rides, galloping, free exercise or working loose, longeing, jumping, schooling, and even showing itself.

At our barn we are fortunate in having a large indoor arena, measuring 200 feet by 120 feet, so that free exercise works easily into our program. Also, because the barn is surrounded by rolling hills, every moment outside helps build the horses' muscles and increases fitness. In the summer months outdoor exercise can really build up horses quickly because they have to move harder and build up more stamina in the heat. We also have miles of hunt and country trails adjacent to our stable so that riders can take their horses for trail rides. In addition, we have several large turnout paddocks, so that all our horses get outside for at least two hours a day.

A horse that has been out of work requires about six weeks to get back into show condition. The most important thing to remember when getting a horse fit is not to overdo it. Develop the horse slowly, increasing the amount of exercise gradually in order to avoid muscle soreness and injury. This possibility is one of the reasons we don't let a horse down completely, but always keep him in light work. This is especially necessary with an older show horse. It is too hard on his body structure to make him work excessively to get fit.

A horse that is shown frequently, especially in the summer months, rarely gets more than a warm-up before a class. He may be given light flat work or longed briefly the morning of a show. A horse that shows infrequently but is sometimes called upon to perform for several consecutive days at a show may need a regular conditioning program to keep him a little soft and relaxed, but fit enough to perform.

Working Loose

A good way to start building endurance and condition in a horse that is either shown infrequently or being brought back is to let him work free in an enclosed area. Working loose is exactly what it sounds like—allowing a horse to move at a trot or canter, without a rider or longe line, around the perimeter of a ring, as shown in Diagram 3.1.

In the case of a horse that hasn't been ridden in a while, you should

C

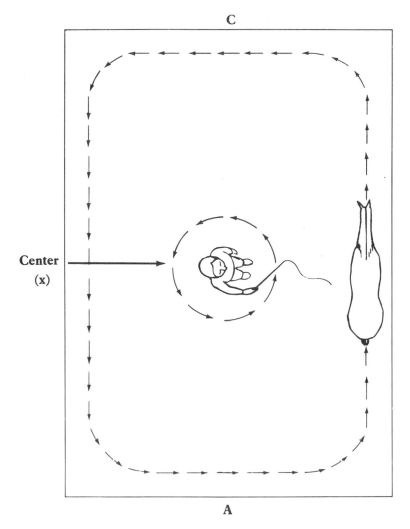

Center
(x)

A

Diagram 3-1. Handler should stand in center of ring and encourage the horse to travel around the perimeter at a steady, easy, gait. Cavallettis can be used to encourage horse to work into the ends of the ring.

begin by having him go only three or four times around the ring or paddock. Don't rush the horse; never force him to canter. You want him to get accustomed to working alone quietly. Start with the horse going along the wall or fence. You don't want to chase or hurry him around with the longe whip, but try to get him moving forward—first with a cluck or hand motion, then by encouraging him with the whip. Sometimes trailing it behind his hocks is enough, and sometimes you have to snap it as a sound cue. Never touch the horse with the whip. You want him to find a steady gait, preferably a trot or a canter. When the horse starts to settle—stop. This is a good time to reverse him and go in the other direction. When conditioning a horse, unless there is a specific problem, always work both directions. By the end of two weeks, the horse should be built up enough to work for about twenty minutes, or about twelve to fifteen laps each way, without getting out of breath or breaking into a sweat. Remember to think in terms of time, because ring size may vary.

Longeing

Longeing is another excellent way to exercise a horse in a controlled fashion, especially one you are bringing back into work, or a young horse in training. It is also ideal for a horse that has been injured. We never turn out a horse who has been stall-rested after an injury without some form of exercise first. The horse is too fresh and can easily overexert and re-injure itself.

As excellent a conditioning tool as longeing can be, it is too much used and abused by unaware horsemen. The handler must know the reasons for longeing a horse. It is not for the inexperienced. We see too many students and teachers longeing horses incorrectly at shows. We don't want to give the impression that longeing is the main way we build horses up. Actually, riding is the best way to condition—but there are times when a need to spare the horse's back or a lack of available riders makes longeing an acceptable substitute. Longeing can also be almost a form of choreography, used to work on and build up specific areas of the horse's anatomy. You have to determine why you are longeing a horse before you decide how long you will do it and what gait you will use.

Longeing puts enormous stress on the legs as the horse is working in a circle in a small area. You have to know your horse's physical limitations.

To longe a horse you will need a longe whip—a nylon longe line that has about a foot and a half of chain shank at the end to clip onto the halter or bridle. Always longe in a leather halter so that it will give way and break if your horse gets in trouble. It is important that your longe line be put away properly (rolled up either in a tight coil or in a figure eight) so that when you go to attach it to the halter, especially if you have a young or fresh horse, you are not dealing with a tangle of nylon lead around your feet and his!

Longeing must be as settled and organized an exercise as possible. Even the way you hold your whip as you walk your horse to the longeing area is significant. Remember, this is a training/conditioning/exercise situation. Hold your whip in your outside hand with the tip trailing down and away from the horse's body. This way, you have free use of your other hand and you can use your whip as a guide.

Make sure you have a suitable area to longe your horse. You need to find a flat, rock-free, soft surface. Make sure the footing is not too deep, as this is worse than hard ground. We use one of our warm-up rings, or the indoor ring when the ground freezes. At a show, you have to be extra careful to choose an area where you will not be cramped and collide with other horses.

Longeing is very much like the discipline of riding. You are aiming for a forward motion. You want to stay behind the shoulder and drive the horse on, leading with the longe line and driving from behind with the whip. Concentrate on keeping the horse going forward along the outside of the circle, away from the center.

We like to start a horse at a slow trot to encourage forward motion. Let the horse out slowly on the longe line, leading him forward and at the same time following him with your other hand and urging him out on the circle. Begin to let the line out and move slightly behind the horse's shoulder and away from him. Don't give him too much line at first. Keep him under control.

Once your line is extended and the horse is moving forward at the end of the line, you may experience a buck or two.

Figure 3.1 shows an early longeing session with a three-year-old horse. This is a potentially explosive situation. The young horse may feel rambunctious and challenge you on the longe line.

Fig. 3-1a. To longe a horse, we use a leather halter over a bridle with an egg-butt snaffle and the reins removed. We attach the longe line to the halter, not to the bit, so that if the horse does something silly, we don't punish his mouth by yanking on the bit. If we anticipate that we may need more control, we lace the chain of the longe line over the horse's nose. Note that the longe whip is trailing down and alongside the horse as a guide while leading him. The horse is properly turned out for longeing, wearing bell boots, galloping boots, and felt hind cuff boots.

Fig. 3-1b. Once you get to the longeing area, lead the horse once around the circle you want him to travel. Let him get acclimated to distractions and assured of the footing. You should check the footing at the same time, especially at a show, where the ground may be unfamiliar. After leading the horse, let him out gradually on the line and start him moving forward at a loose trot.

Fig. 3-1c. Don't get in the habit of being too strong with your whip. First trail the horse with the whip to get him moving forward. A crack is used only to stop a horse from breaking gait or to get him to slow down. Don't constantly resort to verbal clucks, either. If you have trouble keeping the horse out on the circle, point the whip toward his head to lead him back onto it.

Fig. 3-1d. There are three basic points of connection between you and your horse on a longe line: the horse's head, your hand and body, and the tail and longe whip. These should form a V at the apex of your hand and the line. Attach the longe line to the halter ring, holding the line in your hand at about the horse's shoulder, and keeping the longe whip in your other hand, behind the horse's tail.

Fig. 3-1e. This three-year-old was feeling playful, so Frank permitted him a buck or two. But there is a fine line between acceptable playing and ill manners. It is up to the handler to determine. To stop a horse when he gets out of hand or could slip and fall: Pull on the longe line with your hand to steady the horse, making sure you keep your body and hand behind his shoulder. Use verbal cues, such as "whoa," to help settle him.

Fig. 3-1f. Always longe a horse in both directions. When you stop him to go in the other direction, or to rest or change gaits, always walk to him; never allow him to walk in from the circle on his own. Drop your whip, or keep it behind you, as you encourage the horse to turn around and go in the new direction.

Fig. 3-1g. This young horse had trouble going to the left, so we finished up working him one more time to the left as a training procedure.

Horses should come down quietly after a workout, but longeing makes them fresh, so pay particular attention to a horse after a longeing session, especially if he is young or green. He might easily blow up on the way back to the barn.

Always think in terms of time when you are conditioning, especially when longeing. It puts a strain on the horse's legs and should be done for twenty minutes at the most, including walking, trotting, and occasionally galloping, with at least one change of direction. Variations in a routine longeing session are determined by individual needs, but it is a highly effective way to produce overall muscle tone and conditioning if done correctly.

The main object of longeing for conditioning is to keep the horse under control so that he will work his muscles properly. Table 3.1 explains its various purposes and gives some indication of time and method. It is important to consult your trainer or vet about the correctness of your longeing program.

TABLE 3.1
LONGEING

Purpose	Time
Teach green horse discipline	20 minutes. Allow for play. Start in circle at loose trot.
Coming back from injury	Start with 5 minutes at a walk. Build up to 20 minutes in 5-minute increments. Work out program with vet based on type of injury. Vary gaits and direction.
Conditioning	Used in conjunction with working loose and riding. 20-minute session at walk, trot, and canter, with a slow buildup in 5-minute increments.
Substitute for riding/exercise	20 minutes at walk, trot, and canter.
Cold-backed horse (bucks when saddled)	5–10 minutes with tack on, tightening girth at intervals as you longe.
Warm-up at show or suppling exercise	20 minutes—sometimes with bitting rig. This will supple a horse and take the "edge" off him.
Discipline	Specific training maneuver to be formalized with your teacher or trainer. Time, directions and gaits may vary accordingly. 10 minutes in each direction is usual.

Riding

Perhaps the most efficient form of exercise for conditioning is riding itself—in all its many forms—as it incorporates all the exercise disciplines. A horse uses his whole body when he is being ridden and it can be mentally relaxing as well. We are not referring just to serious schooling sessions. A nice trail ride for forty-five minutes, or independent flat work for a half an hour, is a great conditioning exercise when combined with lessons and showing. Some of our very finest show hunters take to the trail a couple of times a week with their riders for a mental and physical unwinding. For a horse being brought back into work, riding on a path with hills and inclines is a natural way to build up endurance and muscles.

Although horses shown frequently are rarely schooled or jumped just before they show, schooling sessions, lessons, and jumping can be good as part of a fitness regime. It is sometimes important for a horse to duplicate in exercise the movements he will be doing in the ring, so as to condition the same sets of muscles. This can be especially useful for an older horse that is shown infrequently. He should be kept in some state of fitness at all times so he does not have to endure a rigorous conditioning regime.

Fig. 3-2. Sometimes a bitting harness or rig is employed when longeing is used as a training exercise. This picture of Playing Games was taken at the 1984 Hampton Classic. Note the folded baby pad at the withers for cushioning under the harness, and the polo wraps and bell boots to protect the front legs.

4

Daily Routines

A victory in the show ring is won as much by the groom as it is by the horse and rider.

The best way to tell you how we get our horses to look the way they do is to invite you back to the barn with us and let you spend the day. The key word at Beacon Hill is *Discipline*. We have a place for everything, and everything is in its place, a way to do everything, and to make sure it is done that way. Sounds a little idealistic? Let us show you how we put it into practice, so you can see how the pieces of our regimen fit together and help us avoid problems.

Each day actually begins the night before, usually around 6 P.M., when we write up a work list covering the complete care of the horse for the next. Grooms and riders are expected to familiarize themselves with the work list before they go home, so that they can organize their day to accomplish what we have set down. In addition, a seven-day chart, as shown in Figure 4.1, organizes the horses' exercise routines.

The objective of our work is to make the horse happy and contented. Everything is done with the horse in mind. That is very important. This is why we have an exceptionally small ratio of grooms to horses—usually three horses to a groom at a show, five at home. We try to assign the same horses to the same grooms both at home and at shows, thereby establishing consistency and a strong rapport between them. A victory in the show ring is won as much by the groom as it is by the horse and rider—at least that's what we think.

In 1984, Beacon Hill sponsored a family day at the International Jumping Derby in Newport, Rhode Island. One of the awards presented was the Groom's Award. We feel strongly about the groom's role in the scheme of things. The groom who won that day is a pretty girl who works for Rhode Island's premier equestrian, Buddy Brown (he, coincidentally, won the Jumping Derby the next day).

27

Beacon Hill

6:30 A.M.	-	Evan feed
6:45 A.M.	-	First 3 horses go out
	-	Salvidor pick up hay, shavings
	-	Stalls cleaned
	-	Water buckets dumped, cleaned, refilled
	-	Horses hayed
	-	Floors swept
	-	Salvidor rake front and back of barn
	-	Bars, grooming boxes, trunks, dusted
	-	Brass polished
	-	Sarah tack room dusted and swept
8:00 A.M.	-	<u>All</u> chores done!
12:00 P.M.	-	Check for hay and water
	-	Floors swept
4:30 P.M.	-	Stalls picked up
	-	Horses hayed, watered
	-	Arturo & Martine wash racks cleaned, dump muck baskets
	-	Sarah tack room
	-	Salvidor pick up hay for P.M. and grain for A.M.
5:00 P.M.	-	Evan feed
	-	Floors swept
	-	Salvidor rake front and back of barn
	-	trunks, etc., dusted
8:30 P.M.- 9:00 P.M.	-	Night chores
	-	Check for hay and water
	-	Sheets, blankets, etc., put on

<u>Horses--September 27-30</u>

<u>Sarah</u>

    Second Step
    Filibuster
    Shakespeare
    Master Dan
    Russian Caviar

<u>Arturo</u>

    Lion in Winter
    Keep On Runnin
    Waiten en Waiten
    Absolutely
    Leave 'em Laughin

<u>Carmelo</u>

    Playing Games
    Dillon
    The Artesian
    Town Talk
    Full Fare

<u>Pennie</u>

    Night Life
    Legacy
    City Lights
    Sunday Best
    Scruples

Fig. 4-1. Beacon Hill work list—made up every night for the next day's chores

We can't say enough good things about our help, and we expect them to have total commitment to the horses they care for. If we take on an apprentice groom, we will pair him or her off with a seasoned groom to learn the Beacon Hill way of doing things.

Becoming a groom is an excellent way to learn about horses, especially if you want to go on and become a trainer. Many of the top trainers and horsemen started as grooms. Here again, tradition is what counts. There is a hierarchy in the horse business—it demands you pay your dues and show your desire to succeed by hard work, never-failing devotion, and a willingness to sacrifice all for the horses. You have to prove yourself to the industry, and, probably even more important, to yourself.

Our grooms all live together in a house we rent about twenty miles from the barn. There is a healthy *espirit de corps* among them as they live, talk, and breathe horses together.

Through the Day

A typical day at Beacon Hill starts at 6:30 A.M., but very often a groom will set the alarm early and beat the others up to the barn to make sure his horses get to the turnout paddocks first, before feeding. Feeding is between 6:30 and 7:00 A.M., and we try to stay on schedule when we're home. This does as much for keeping a horse fat and healthy as anything. Feeding is always done by one person, usually the barn manager. We post stall cards with a feed chart for every horse. Before they are grained, they are given a slice of hay and fresh water.

Horses are creatures of habit. They expect things to be done in a certain way and come to look for them. A new horse at our barn may actually go "off his feed" and put his ears back for the first few weeks until he adjusts to the new routine. Once the horses know that feeding is on schedule, a groom can come in early and take his horse out to the paddocks with nary a nicker for hay from the others. They know the routine.

On a typical day, a groom who wants to get an early start will arrive at the barn around 5:30 A.M. Before walking his horses to the paddock, he first picks out their feet (in the stalls, to keep droppings out of the aisleways). If you remember to pick out your horse's feet first thing every morning until it becomes a habit, you will go a long way toward preventing one of the most insidious hoof diseases—thrush.

After picking out his horses' feet, the groom puts each of them on cross ties and knocks them off—a quick brushing. If the weather is warm the horses will be turned out without a rug, but in spring and fall they wear a New Zealand rug. Our horses also always wear bell boots and galloping boots or polo wraps when they're turned out and for work. The polo wraps and galloping boots protect the tendons and shins from injury, and the bell boots guard the heel and bulb. Making sure the horses are turned out every day when they are not showing is a very important facet of our care and fitness program. We believe in making the horses feel good. They need to get out, feel free, and roll and stretch out the kinks. At a show where turnout is impossible, we make sure the horses get light exercise, dictated by individual needs.

Ideally, a groom's horses stay in the paddocks for a couple of hours while he mucks out their stalls and hays and waters the barn. Sometime later in the day, he may snatch a half hour and take one of them out for a grazing walk.

At 7 A.M. the grooms bring their horses in for feeding. Now the aisleway is bustling with activity. It sometimes looks to us like the deck of a ship as the horses are stationed on cross ties while the grooms work around them, removing night bandages and blankets and brushing them off and checking them over. The nuts-and-bolts work of the day is done at this time. Then the barn manager wheels the feed cart down the aisleway, and soon all you hear is the comforting sound of munching horses. The aisleways are cleared and the grooms spend that half hour or so attending to chores, tidying up their stations, sorting out dirty laundry to be sent out, rolling bandages—the hundred details that make their day run smoothly.

After feeding, the horses are groomed before beginning their day's assignments. The first grooming of the day is typical of how we do it at Beacon Hill. (See also illustrated, step-by-step grooming session on pages 32–34.) The horse is placed on cross ties, with grooming tools easily at hand. (When a groom first comes to work at Beacon Hill, we supply him with a leather grooming halter and lead shank, a grooming and a bandage box, and anything else we feel he needs to do the job right. Any special requisitions are gladly filled. The grooms are responsible for their grooming stations and supplies.)

The horse will already have had his leg bandages, if any, removed. (We usually don't wrap our horses unless there is a problem.) The next step is to lift the dirt out of the horse's coat by rubbing in circular motions against the hair. Most grooms prefer a grooming mitt (a rubber mitten with nubs, like a Swedish bath mitt) for this, but some use a curry comb— a hard rubber, ridged, or small-toothed comb. After rubbing or currying the horse, many grooms will vacuum him to remove loose dirt and hair, although you can also do this with a stiff-bristled brush. Then they take a soft finishing brush and brush in the direction of the hair to smooth down and polish the coat. Finally they polish the coat with a rub rag or towel.

This rubbing is the secret of good grooming and is important for producing show horses that shimmer, as the rubbing releases the oil in the hair follicles. There is absolutely no substitute for rub power! The rub rag or towel is omnipresent at a horse show, tucked into the back pocket of a groom's jeans, as shown in Figure 4.2. In the morning, a groom will rub a horse for about fifteen minutes if his coat is already perfect. Otherwise it could take between forty-five minutes and two hours. A groom once turned to Marion Hulick and asked her, "What do I do about this horse—he keeps on shedding?" Marion retorted, "Keep rubbing on him until there is no hair left." It took another two hours. The trick to rubbing is to do it every day so that no hair fills in. Our horses have glistening, oil-toned coats and there is not an extra hair on them. However, some horses are so fine-skinned, especially chestnuts, that you have to be careful you don't actually rub a bald spot.

After brushing and polishing, horses that have had poultices on will be taken to the wash stall to have their legs washed off. (All the horses' legs are washed after work, during the final grooming of the day.) The legs must be dried thoroughly. Wet legs are a primary cause of scratches.

Scratches are the bane of the horse world. Wet patches behind the horse's heels get caked with stall dust or mud from the paddock. A skin infection erupts in the sore and splits the skin in the tender hide behind the heel. The result looks just like deep cat scratches. You can imagine how uncomfortable this can be for a hunter or jumper as he lifts his legs

Fig. 4-2. The rub rag is omnipresent at a horse show. Here it is tucked into the back pocket of a groom's jeans. Notice the leather and chain lead shank worn around the waist. Grooms devise exceedingly clever ways to carry their tools on their person so as to be ready for any emergency.

over a jump and squeezes these sore folds together. It sometimes makes the legs so tender that the horses don't even want to lift their legs, so they walk lame.

Here's where a good groom can be invaluable. One of our grooms alerted us to scratches forming on one of our best jumpers after the Lake Placid show, held at the end of July. We were able to dry them up in a matter of days, in time for a major show four weeks later. If the groom hadn't spotted them early, the scratches might have advanced too far for us to be able to do this.

Once a horse is groomed and checked for any blemishes or other problems, his groom either tacks him for flat work or a lesson, longes him, lets him work loose, or does whatever else the work chart calls for. This is another important aspect of our program to build condition and keep our horses contented. We make sure they get some kind of free exercise or individualized workout every day. Even when we let a horse down in between shows, we will never take him entirely out of work, pulling his shoes and completely letting him down. Our horses are athletes and champions. They get used to using their bodies and can actually pine away if left to stand and do nothing. And strenuous conditioning is hard on their constitution if they're really unfit, so continuous light work is useful even for horses that don't have a rigorous show schedule.

Grooming

Step by Step

When you begin grooming, your horse may be coated with heavy dirt from rolling, lying in his stall, etc. First determine how to get the bulk dirt off. You may need to give him a bath or vacuum him first. If a horse is sweaty, a bath or a rinse-off is best, but if you don't bathe him, let his hair dry thoroughly before going on with:

the curry comb. This hard-ridged or rubber-bristled oval tool is used to lift out the dirt and sweat salt. Use brisk circular motions against the hair all over the body of the horse, avoiding the bony surfaces. For these you use:

the rubber curry mitt. This rubber mitten is covered with nubs much like those on a Swedish bath mitt and is used on the skeletal areas

Fig. 4-3. Grooming essentials – all you will need to get the job done: hoof pick *
hoof packing for packing caulks, and sore soles * Corona for applying to coronet
band to help grow smooth feet * baby oil * alcohol in spray bottle for sore tendons
and removing stains * fly spray * hoof dressing * No More Tangles for manes and
tails * Vaseline * sponge for wetting manes and tails * stiff wire brush for getting
dirt off hooves * rubber mitt * curry comb * hard and soft brushes * Ace bandages
for tail wraps * rub rag or towel.

such as the legs and face. Many grooms also use it on the whole body in
place of the curry comb. After currying, use:

the body brush. This is a stiff-bristled brush that is used to brush off
loose dirt. Save tender areas such as the face for:

the dandy brush. This is a soft-bristled brush that is used on the face
and legs and to smooth down the horse's coat as a final touch. After
brushing, many grooms then wash the legs with Ivory or a mild, aloe-
based soap—rinse and dry thoroughly. Then reach for the:

rub rag or towel. The rub rag is used to lift the oil in the horse's coat
to the surface and, literally, polish him. It also helps blood circulation and
removes loose hairs. If the horse has not been given a bath, or if he will not
be braided the next day, the groom might then wash the horse's tail in a
shampoo such as No More Tangles. Then, always use:

the water brush. This is a stiff-bristled brush used to wet down a horse's mane after tacking up or work or before retiring him for the night. It is an excellent tool for training a mane to lie flat and is also used on the tops of tails. Dip the brush through water and pass through hair. A damp sponge may also be used for this purpose. Next:

clean the face. This is a much-forgotten part of grooming. Wipe out moist, dirty areas such as the nostrils and around the eyes and ears with a damp or dry towel. Before a show, you can apply a little baby oil around the eyes and muzzle for a glistening, alert expression. A grooming session always ends with:

painting the hooves. A thin coating of hoof oil is brushed on.

After grooming, a horse will either be tacked for show or exercise, or put away for the night. Any special procedures, such as medication or bandaging, are also attended to at this time.

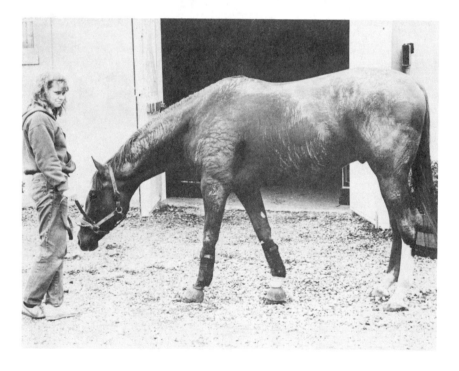

Fig. 4-4a. Grooming: Believe it or not, this is how our horses can look after they have been turned out for a good healthy roll. (We don't want you to think we keep them stalled and immaculate at all times.)

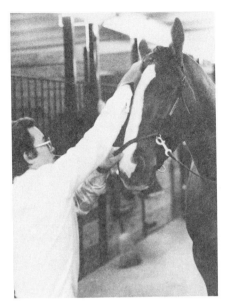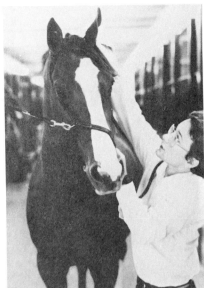

Fig. 4-4b (left). Most grooms prefer a rubber grooming mitt to a curry comb. It is ideal for all-over removal of dirt, but is especially designed for use on the sensitive skeletal areas of the horse such as his legs and face.

Fig. 4-4c (right). The rub rag is used to raise the oils to the skin's surface, and to rub off loose hair. It is the secret behind Beacon Hill's flawless and shimmering coats and is also excellent for cleaning moist and sensitive areas such as ears, mouth, eyes, and nostrils. After approximately forty-five minutes of grooming, this horse will be ready to show, school, or put to bed.

Bathing

Bathing is essential to our grooming program—especially at shows, where we might be handling as many as thirty horses at a time. We bathe our horses frequently, for good hygiene and to prevent irritation caused by the buildup of sweat, dust, and dirt. (See Table 4.1, Bathing Chart.) We try not to bathe more than three times a week, however, since too much bathing can dry out the natural oils in the horse's coat and leave it dry and dull. We are always careful to use only very mild soap and warm water, sometimes with oil added. There are several reasons for this: (1) the comfort of the horse—*you* try taking a cold shower after a hard workout; (2) a horse can tie up—get an advanced state of muscle cramps—from

Table 4.1
BATHING

Basics

Type of application	Reason	Frequency	Products used
Soap and water	To clean dirt and sweat	As needed; not to exceed 3 times a week	Ivory or a mild or aloe-based soap.
Body brace	Relieve tired and sore muscles	Every time worked	Vetrolin, or similar liniment
Iodine/medicated soap	Clear up secondary skin infections such as ringworm, rain blisters	As needed	Weladol, Betadine (mild iodine soaps)
Fungicide	To treat fungus, a common condition in warm climates	As needed	DeFungit spray, Captan, Colloidal soap, fungicides
Hot oil	To condition and make a coat shiny	As needed	Hot oil (corn or baby oil) added to warm water

having cold water applied to his warm body, combined with the chill of the wind; (3) mild, aloe-based soap will not cause fine-skinned horses to blister (develop burns and blotches on the skin caused by abrasion and irritation); (4) heat is one of the secrets of creating a shiny coat. There are hot oil treatments for human hair, to repair damage and add luster and body, and the same technique works for horses. The more often heat is

Cosmetics/Enhancers
(apply as needed)

Coat type/ color/other	Problems	Product used
Gray	Hard to get lustrous; turns yellow, stains easily from saddle leather	Laundry blueing, human hair blueing rinse, e.g., Lady Clairol
White legs	Hard to keep clean; must look perfectly white for show purposes	Ivory soap preferred; some use Bon Ami
Thin mane	Breaks off easily; grows unevenly	Wash separately with soap; apply cream rinse
Thick mane	Coarse hair, tends to stand up; grows in layers	Wet down with sponge often so that it will train itself to lie flat. Training braids are sometimes used. (See *Braiding*.) Comb when wet.
Thin coat	Blisters easily, rubs off leaving bald spot	Don't bathe as often or use harsh products. Be careful of too much fly spray, Vetrolin liniments, and excessive grooming.

---

applied to a horse's coat, through warm water, blankets, or friction from a rub rag, the more the coat will shine from natural oils and improved circulation.

We have a shower stall with a drain. The cement floor is covered with rubber matting. We usually use several buckets of warm water, rather than a hose, to wash and rinse the horses.

Fig. 4-5. The Shower Stall. Plastic milk crates mounted at hand level make for ease of operation. Bathing essentials: body liniment (Vetrolin) * DeFungit in a plastic atomizer to treat fungus * Weladol or tame iodine soap * Ivory soap for bathing whole body or legs * cream rinse for tangles in mane and tail * blueing for gray horses * Pinesol disinfectant to wash shower stall periodically to prevent growth of fungus and bacteria. Aids: cross ties * rubber matting * drain * hose with hot and cold water * natural sponges * sweat scraper * whirlpool for soaking

First, fill a bucket with warm, soapy water. You may add Vetrolin or any other type of body liniment directly to this, or apply it separately as a body brace, as shown in the photograph that follows. Sponge on soapy

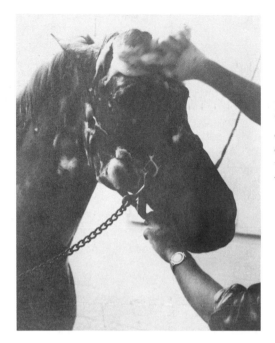

Fig. 4-6. The key to a proper bath is to wet the horse thoroughly and then lather him all over, remembering to get between legs and on the face, where a horse sweats the most.

water and work it right into the coat. Then take a sweat scraper and take off the excess soap and water. Now comes a two-bucket rinse. Saturate the sponge with water and leave it dripping wet. Squeeze in a sweeping motion over the horse from top to bottom. Gravity will help out and the water will run down, covering large portions of the horse. Rinse twice, using two buckets.

Should you wish to add a body brace in addition to washing the horse, sponge on a mixture made of two ounces of Vetrolin, or a similar liniment, to a bucket of water, then scrape and let dry. (Some of our grooms do not like the residue this leaves on the coat and prefer to rinse it off. One of our most experienced grooms uses only a cupful of alcohol in the rinse water, which he claims soothes and tones muscles like a human body brace but evaporates, leaving nothing in the coat to interfere with grooming.)

In addition to bathing the horses approximately three times a week and giving them body braces almost daily, we deal with problem spots such as manes, tails, and legs more frequently. Legs are rinsed daily to get sand and mud off and white legs get a heavy-duty scrub. Manes and tails are washed often to keep dirt and dandruff from building up, and to keep them full and healthy. Braiding is hard on a horse's mane and tail, and keeping them clean and groomed is about the only thing you can do to prevent them from getting brittle and breaking off. Sometimes a cream rinse is used to condition them and to get rid of tangles.

Cleaning the Sheath

Cleaning the sheath is an important part of horse hygiene that can be aggravating to the animal and distasteful to the groom or horse owner. However, it must be done on a routine basis for the comfort and well-being of the horse. The sheath needs to be washed because over months of showing and stabling, dust and dirt collect at the opening of the sheath where it encloses the penis. In addition, a waxy substance called smegma is secreted in this area and with the accumulated dust and dirt can build up to form an uncomfortable mass. In extreme cases the horse will have difficulty letting down his penis to urinate and a swollen and infected sheath can develop.

A groom or horseman who is paying proper attention to his animal will know when it is time to clean a sheath, but a good rule of thumb is to do it every few months.

To clean the sheath, use warm water and a mild soap. Have a small sponge and towel on hand. Cross-tie the horse if possible (we clean the horse's sheath in our shower stall, which has them), as you may need some restraint. Approach with caution. Our horses are quite accustomed to this procedure, but for an uncertain horse you may need to use a humane twitch, or ask your vet to tranquilize him. When a horse is tranquilized he relaxes and allows the penis to drop down, so cleaning is made easier. If the sheath has not been cleaned for a long time or is excessively dirty, coat the penis and inside of the sheath with Vaseline and let it soften the waxy buildup for a few hours before washing.

To wash, insert your hand into the sheath and gently soap the area, working the accumulation of dirt and smegma loose. Continue doing this until the area is thoroughly clean and free of any matter. If your horse is used to cleaning, he may let you rinse the inside of the sheath with a hose (use warm water). If not, use a wet sponge with clean, warm water. Be sure to rinse the area completely.

Care of Chestnuts

The chestnuts are found on the inside of the front and hind legs above the knee, and should be kept level with the hair on the leg. It is easiest to scrape them down when they have been softened by a bath, so most of our grooms chip them off with a fingernail or blunt knife about once a week when bathing a horse.

Finishing Touches

Before a horse is returned to his stall at the end of the day after being bathed, the groom may apply bandages if needed (see Chapter 5), hoof oil, and/or Corona dressing to the coronet band from which the hoof grows. This antiseptic dressing with an animal-fat base is used primarily for cuts and scrapes, but its healing and softening properties stimulate hoof growth and repair. The key to good grooming is preventative care. By applying hoof dressing and hoof oil daily, you will alleviate the problems of hoof cracks, chipping, and dryness (Figure 4.7).

Sometimes there can be too much of a good thing. It used to be a barn rule that hoof oil be applied every time a horse was worked. We found that the horse's feet were actually getting too brittle, and we now try to do it less often, usually once a day, except at a show, where hoof oil is applied everytime a horse goes into the ring—even when he is asked to jog for soundness.

Fig. 4-7. To grow smooth hooves, apply Corona in a 1-inch strip around coronet band where hair meets foot. The hoof will grow in smooth and crack free.

Equipment and Good Grooming

Cleanliness of the horses' appointments is another aspect of good grooming. Our tack is cleaned and checked for repairs daily, while the horses are being used, or when the grooms have a spare moment. Grooms are responsible for cleaning bridles and riders their own saddles and girths. Local tack shops and craftsmen keep tack and bits in good repair. Most saddle and girth rubs and sores are caused by dirty, sweat-soaked horse pads and girth covers. Sweat contains salt, and the buildup of this abrasive chemical, combined with dirt, in pads and blankets plays havoc with hair follicles. Rubs begin to show, and soon infections set in. Dirty pads and blankets can also spread fungus and other skin infections from horse to horse.

Beacon Hill produces two hefty bags of dirty laundry each day—baby pads (small quilted mattresses), bandages, towels, and sheets. Large loads are sent out to a local laundry; small loads are done at the barn. If you do your own laundry, remember to use only mild detergent and very little bleach, and rinse twice to get the soap out. Any soap residue or bleach that is left in baby or saddle pads can combine with the horses' sweat and blister them, especially horses like ours, who are so well groomed that they are practically hairless.

At the end of the day, the grooms go over their charges once more and look for any injuries—cuts, scrapes, rub marks, or swellings. A groom's main job is to prevent a problem from developing—to treat a swelling before it becomes big knee; medicate a cut before it blossoms into an infection; pad a rub before it becomes a saddle or girth sore. We take full responsibility, with our barn manager, for medicating horses and calling the vet.

After the final checkup the barn is fed, usually between 5 P.M. and 6 P.M., depending on the time of year and the schedule. The horses are then bedded down for the night. Most are blanketed. During the hottest days of the summer they may get just a sheet, or nothing, but in serious cold they may get a blanket, a wool liner, and another blanket on top. The weight keeps the horses' coats flat and the warmth keeps them from growing out, so they stay sleek and shiny.

After feeding there is a last water and stall check. The barn is tidied up and swept, and everyone leaves for the day. The barn manager sleeps in an apartment over the barn, so he is never far away. He makes a barn visit at 11 P.M. to check on water buckets and hay and to add or remove blankets as needed. The grooms live in a nearby house. Everyone on staff is within twenty minutes of the farm.

We have shown you a typical day at Beacon Hill. When we arrive at a

Fig. 4-8. Wheelbarrows lined up alongside Beacon Hill barn.

show, we try to continue with our daily routines so that everything runs like clockwork, and the horses feel contented and secure in a home-away-from-home environment. As days run into nights, as class after class, warm-up after warm-up session is dealt with, only the horses stay close to schedule.

Turning Out a Horse Not Stabled at Beacon Hill

Some of our top junior competitors, for reasons of logistics and choice, are not able to stable their horses at Beacon Hill. They show under our tutelage and van their horses to the barn on a regular basis for lessons. In these cases we are especially concerned that riders maintain the standards we have set and arrive at a show with their horses turned out the way we insist on. We are proud to say that they seldom fail in this endeavor, which just goes to prove that anyone can turn out a horse to these exacting standards without a staff of grooms, professional braiders, and others.

Riders of ours who stable outside Beacon Hill accept responsibility for having their horses ready for and entered in a show. Of course, we are in constant touch with them, but it is basically up to them, and their families, to have their horse fit to show.

Perhaps the most shining example of a home-stabling program that helps make for a winner in the show ring is that of our student Francesca Mazella of Mount Kisco, New York, who is helped by her devoted mother. Francesca is one of the leading junior riders in the nation today. In 1984, she won *both* the AHSA Medal and the Maclay, becoming the first young rider to do so in eighteen years. She also won a United States Equestrian Team gold medal, which entails winning twenty USET classes. At only fifteen years of age, Francesca has been featured in *Seventeen* magazine and *Practical Horseman* as a possible future USET contender. She is supremely motivated and professional, and takes care of her two champion hunter/jumpers, Rugged Rule and Free Union, including braiding them, by herself. This is in addition to the long hours she puts in schooling, taking lessons, and showing.

Fig. 4-9. Francesca Mazella of Mount Kisco, New York, all smiles as she leads her gelding Rugged Rule across the schooling area at the 1984 Hampton Classic in Bridgeport, New York, two months before she won the AHSA medal in September 1984, and the Maclay in November 1984, becoming the first junior rider to do so in eighteen years.

At the Mazellas', the day begins at 5:45 A.M. on school days, when Francesca goes to the barn to feed the horses and muck out the stalls.

Because the Mazellas have a mixed bag of horses, from ancient ponies (one was ridden by her mother), to top hunters and jumpers, they feed a well-rounded mix of pellets, Omolene (sweet feed) and whole oats. This mixture has less protein than some—about 10 percent altogether. They feed alfalfa hay and add corn oil and gelatin to the feed to promote shiny coats and non-brittle hooves, respectively. They also put electrolytes in the water, and use iodized salt licks. The Mazellas attempt to keep a schedule at home similar to that at Beacon Hill. Feedings are always at the same time. The horses get a slice of hay at lunch, and an evening feed around 6:00 P.M., when lessons, flat work, and chores are done. Patricia Mazella, Francesca's mother, who is a horsewoman in her own right, does the careful job a good groom would do.

The Mazellas have twelve acres for their personal horse facility and have grazing land adjacent to their property. This means the horses are able to be turned out. Mrs. Mazella gets to the barn at about 9 A.M. and grooms the horses before turning them out. Although she, too, tries not to bathe her horses too often, giving them instead a Vetrolin bath rinse-off, she has the awesome task of keeping a gray horse, Free Union, free of stains and yellowing. She uses Quick Silver, a blueing hair rinse for people, and carries a bottle of alcohol for spot cleaning.

Patricia Mazella is one of the sharpest grooms around and is constantly on the lookout for surefire cure-alls. Once, when one of the Mazellas' prized hunters got scratches in the middle of the show season and they needed an overnight cure, she unearthed a mixture of A & D ointment, cortisone, and Furacin, blended in equal parts, from friendly grooms. Rugged Rule has an extremely high wither, and to prevent rubs she pins a baby pad into the lining of his blanket where it meets the wither (using a large safety pin and folding the ends under), and foam padding under his saddle. Because this can be unsightly, she has made a slipcover for it of simulated sheepskin. If a rub does occur, she treats it with mineral oil to keep it soft, and also uses Furacin for scrapes and sores.

Francesca does her own braiding, with strict attention to the Beacon Hill rule of black or dark yarn. When her horse arrives for a lesson or at the ring to show, he is turned out properly—hooves oiled, braids and tail perfect, coat rubbed to a sheen, boots polished to a mirrored perfection. There are no shortcuts to good grooming, and the Mazellas may start at 3:30 in the morning to make a class at 8 A.M.

5

Special Maintenance

The three things that are hardest on the feet of hunters and jumpers are water, longeing, and shipping.

—George Fitzgerald
farrier

If we were to summarize our objectives in maintaining show horses, we'd say that we are constantly fighting changes: changes in weather, ground, horse show conditions, equine general health, soundness, and appearance. Every day brings with it an evaluation of how to maintain the status quo: how to ensure that a strenuous workout doesn't develop into sore or swollen tendons; that an unexpected drop in the temperature doesn't encourage a horse's coat to grow; that feet are shod every four to six weeks and are able to withstand the rigors of jumping without breaking or cracking under pressure. Fighting changes and implementing an offensive program of maintenance and prevention, as opposed to a defensive one of correction and problem solving, are the working goals of our staff, as they should be for every horse owner.

Hoof Care and Shoeing

It takes eleven months for a horse to grow a foot, and six months for him to shed a frog. These are the parameters you are dealing with when you think about long-term correction of any problem in this area.

The biggest foot problem we have in our barn is thrush, a bacterial infection that thrives along the crevices of the hoof's frog. The bacteria live in the ground, and when the horse's foot becomes packed with stall

Fig. 5-1. Farrier George Fitzgerald from Glastonbury, Connecticut, who comes to our barn an average of once a week and travels with us on the circuit

matter and manure, it becomes a fertile area for the infection to set in, especially in the damp. One of the difficulties in a show barn is that the horses are in their stalls a lot, and their feet are in water much of the time, as they are washed and hosed down frequently. This creates ideal conditions for thrush, which is why we are so fanatical about having our horses' feet picked out first thing each morning. We treat thrush at the first sign of decay by squirting medicine into the grooves of the frog, and, as in all aspects of our maintenance program, we turn to the experts, such as our blacksmith, George Fitzgerald. George is a third-generation farrier from Glastonbury, Connecticut, who travels the A show circuit and shoes for competitive show barns from Maine to Florida.

What most people don't realize is that thrush encompasses both a fungus and a bacteria. When you encounter a stubborn case of thrush that appears unresponsive to the usual thrush remedies like Coppertox, it is probably because you are not treating the fungus as well. The fungus is a crusty varmint that feeds on the dead frog cells. One of the best treatments for fungus is iodine, and I find that soaking the foot in Betadine iodine solution works well. Be sure to dry the foot after you soak it.

Before I doctor thrush, I trim away the rough pieces of the atrophied hoof around the frog and cut out whatever pockets have formed where the thrush and fungus have eaten holes in the foot. The horses are usually shod with pads, but we leave them off while there is a thrush problem. Then we clean the holes and grooves in the foot thoroughly, using a tongue depressor and cotton gauze pads—never a hoof pick (Figure 5.2). Then I am ready to doctor the hoof with a thrush remedy. I don't recommend harsh treatments because they tend to burn the tissue instead of treating the bacterial infection. A horse can get foot-sore with a bad case of thrush. When the heels shift slightly as a horse moves, friction is caused in the area that's affected by a deep case of thrush. Bar shoes can help a really bad case from causing discomfort by taking the weight off the heels and distributing it evenly over more surface.

My favorite hoof dressing is a mixture of cod liver oil and Fiebing's hoof dressing. Cod liver oil draws flies, but the smell of the Fiebing's shoos them away. I know that a show horse gets hoof dressing painted on more often than it should, for appearance' sake, so try to apply it lightly.

There are two objectives to applying hoof dressing: to promote growth and to stimulate growth. Promoting naturally healthy growth of the hoof is usually the objective, but if the hoof has been damaged or is cracked, we may want to stimulate it. The lanolin found in any animal-based hoof product promotes growth of the horn. One that is often preferred is Corona, which is made from the fat of sheep. Corona applied daily

Fig. 5-2. Thrush treatment: After trimming away the atrophied hoof and cutting away the pockets caused by the thrush, George will take a piece of gauze and push it gently through the grooves next to the frog to clean out the area. *Never use a hoof pick*, as the foot will be sore.

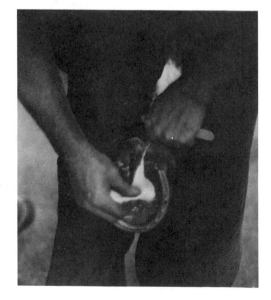

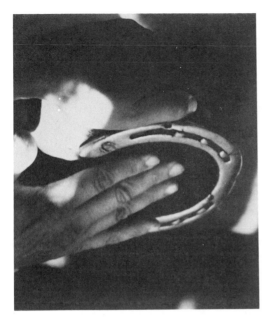

Fig. 5-3. Packing the sole: Forshner's Medicated Hoof Packing with a pine tar base is used to help draw out soreness and provide cushioning for tender soles, stone bruises, and on hard ground.

in a one-inch strip around the coronet band where the hair meets the hoof will work wonders, making smooth, crack-free, strong new hooves. An old-fashioned mixture, favored when harness horses were used every day, is pine tar and bacon fat. My father used this mixture on his harness horses.

The three things that are hardest on the feet of hunters and jumpers are water, longeing, and shipping. We've discussed water—there is, unavoidably, too much of it. Longeing puts considerable pressure on the hooves and can cause them to break up and shoes to wear out. Four weeks is about the longest hunters on the circuit can wear one set of shoes. Shipping is perhaps hardest on a horse's feet. Shoes are pried off in transit and coronet bands are clipped in crowded quarters. Shipping bandages dropped down to the coronet band help protect the area. We also pack our horses' feet with pine tar hoof packing to help draw out soreness and cushion soles over long distances (Figure 5.3).

Pine tar is one of those natural remedies that can accomplish a lot of things. It can draw out soreness, so it is a marvelous ingredient in hoof packing, and it is also an excellent material to use when putting pads on a horse that has a stone bruise. When mixed with oakum it hardens to act as a cushion.

Stone bruises are another common complaint of show horses that have to jump in all sorts of rings and practice areas. A stone bruise is really a blood vessel that has ruptured on sharp contact. To treat a bruise, we first pull the shoe and attempt to locate the bruise by cutting away the sole. After pulling the shoe, we soak the foot in Epsom salts and apply a poultice to draw out soreness. There are several good commercial poultices on the market, but a traditional favorite is bran mixed with warm water. It's messy, though. You can also use Ichthammol packed in with cotton.

Shelly hoof is another equine dilemma blacksmiths have to deal with. A shelly hoof is one that scales off and breaks up at the bottom and around the nail holes, making for a poor appearance. It is more common among quarter horses, and horses that are out a lot and get dry, hard feet from exposure. I have found that putting on pads really helps because they hold in packing and allow its moisture to seep into the foot. Pads help strengthen the bars of the foot and put pressure on the frog, which stimulates circulation. They also help the hoof withstand pressure—another principal cause of shelly hooves.

Common sense applies when it comes to hoof care. I get annoyed when a groom or horse owner applies hoof dressing and then runs a horse across dirt before it dries. Hoof dressing is important as a grooming aid, because it darkens the hooves and makes the surface appear uniform, giving the horse a finished look. (Hunters and jumpers don't have black polish put on their hooves as is done in the quarter horse, halter and pleasure, and saddlebred worlds.) If your horse is shod with wide-web aluminum plates, be sure to keep hoof dressing away from the shoes; a chemical reaction with aluminum builds up a corroding substance that makes the shoes pull away from the foot. However, a mixture of cod liver oil and Feibing's won't do this. As another enhancer of style and appearance, when I finish off a shoeing job, I fill in the holes in the hoof with plastic wood sealer which wears away gradually as the hoof grows.

Fig. 5-4. Hoof care essentials: all you will need to keep the horse's feet in good repair. Fiebing's hoof dressing ∗ Forshner's hoof packing ∗ stiff brush to clean out dirt ∗ hoof oil with paintbrush ∗ thrush remedy ∗ hoof pick ∗ bell boots and hind felt cuffs to protect horse from interfering

Caulks: For Sure Footing

When shoeing one of our horses, our farrier will drill eight holes in the shoes—one in each heel—to hold the caulks (Figure 5.5). One of the first things we do when we arrive at a show is determine the condition of the footing. Then, before the horse is schooled or performs, the groom and trainer will decide what length caulks, if any, are needed. The decision takes into account the speed of the course, the fences, and the horse's weight. Caulks can give a horse the traction he needs on the turf or dirt if it is soft. In general, we use smaller caulks on the front shoes, larger ones behind. After a certain amount of time on the circuit, we've come to expect certain conditions at certain shows.

As with everything else, there is a right way to take care of caulks and caulk holes. Shortly after a horse has finished working, the caulks are removed and the holes are packed with cotton. We are adamant about this. With caulks in, it is easy for a horse to step on and cut himself. Also, on the hard ground outside the ring, they can change the angle at which a horse stands. If the holes are packed immediately, you do not have to remove bedding and manure to reset the caulks.

Fig. 5-5. Caulks are screwed into the eight holes drilled out by the blacksmith in the heels of the horses' shoes. They provide better footing at shows. To keep the caulks and holes well oiled and rust free, store the caulks in a plastic container with oil and drop cotton in the holes before you pack them.

Caulks should be kept in oil. A small plastic container with just enough cooking or baby oil to cover the caulks works well. This keeps the threads from rusting. Also, if you drop your cotton in oil just before you pack the caulk holes, when you remove the cotton, the grooves are oiled and screwing in the caulks is much easier. Most grooms use a shoeing nail to clean out caulk holes and an adjustable wrench to screw the caulks in.

Bandaging

Proper bandaging is a science. It takes a lot of deliberation because once you've started to bandage a horse you can cause his legs to become dependent on the wraps and instigate rebound problems. Tendons lose elasticity from too much tightening through bandaging, and they harden and thicken instead. We try first to prevent tendon and leg problems from developing by correct workouts and careful attention to changes in the horses' legs. Some bandages are designed to help prevent problems from occurring. Others are for healing and involve special treatments.

You have to treat every horse as an individual when it comes to bandaging. There are no hard-and-fast rules. We depend on the grooms to notice any hot spots or puffiness on the tendons or suspensory ligaments and report them to us. We, in turn, keep in mind what kind of workout and/or show schedule a horse is going to have and tell the grooms how and when to bandage. We also rely on our grooms to make bandaging decisions on their own in the day-to-day care of the horse.

Some bandages are protective, for example, shipping bandages and polo wraps. Some, such as rundown bandages, are supportive. Others, such as poultice, sweat, or spider bandges, are used to heal injuries. Below are some common bandage types and how and when they are applied (always within 40 minutes to insure therapeutic value).

Standing bandage. One of the most regularly used bandages, this can be employed for many purposes: with extended flannels or cottons for shipping; alone as a soft support; with a body brace to tighten tendons; with a cooling gel to reduce swelling; or as a covering to a poultice or a sweat or blister.

Shipping bandage. Basically a standing bandage, as described above, with the cottons extended below an inch or two to the bulb of the heel and above just to the knee to add further protection, flannel bandages covering the cottons. We do not use shipping boots because they do not offer the support to the tendons that shipping bandages do. We may add bell boots if we think we need further protection for the coronet band area.

Fig. 5-6. Bandaging essentials: a sampling of the many items you should have on hand to bandage effectively. Uptite poultice * cotton sheets * flannel bandages * alcohol in spray atomizer * tape * safety pins * brown paper ovals * cooling gels

Polo wrap. Used for schooling, showing, and turnout simply as a protective covering and light support for the shin and tendon. We prefer a dark or black polo wrap for uniformity of appearance and because it is less distracting. To put on a polo wrap, start at the top of the lower leg, below the knee, and wrap down the leg from front to back around the tendon. Fasten with the Velcro closing, safety pins, or tape.

Support bandage (Figure 5.7). Applied to tighten the pores of the tendons and cool the legs down before or after an unusually heavy workout or show, which may produce muscle soreness. Before applying the bandage you can also rub the lower legs with alcohol (rub briskly up and down against the hair), which also cools and tightens as it evaporates, and apply a thin coating of a cooling gel such as EAF Blue Gel.

Rundown bandage (Figure 5.8). Adds support and protection to the ankle and tendon. We use Kendall cotton, Ace bandages, and safety pins or elastic tape for this type of bandage. Kendall cotton works well because it stretches and can be molded to the leg. The bandage may be used with splint boots for further support of the tendons and ankles. A horse that is shown in rundowns may be schooled or worked in polo wraps so that he doesn't get too dependent on the support.

Fig. 5-7a (above left). The support or stable bandage: Start with a clean, dry leg, with the hair brushed down evenly. Spray alcohol on leg and work into hair. Wrap padded cottons around leg, starting between cannon bone and tendon in middle of leg, wrapping front to back.

Fig. 5-7b (above right). Wrap flannels around cotton starting in the middle of leg and working down, then up to the top. Wrap front to back, as with cottons.

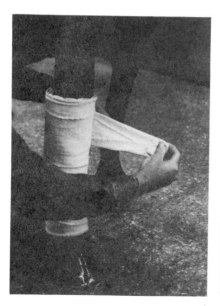 

Fig. 5-7c (left). For a neat finish, fold in sides of flannel one half inch and fold end two to three inches.

Fig. 5-7d (right). Pin bandage, or secure with tape. Make sure tape is not too tight or you can cause a knot on the tendon, known as "cording."

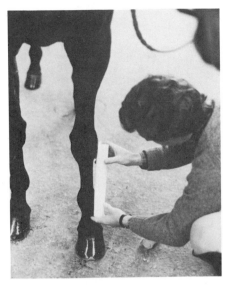

Fig. 5-8a (left). The rundown bandage: First, measure your horse's leg by laying cotton beside lower leg. Bandage should come from just below the knee to the point of the ankle.

Fig. 5-8b (right). To start wrapping, place the cotton between the cannon bone and the tendon on the inside of the leg. You do not want the seam to end on the tendon or cannon bone, but between them on the outside of the leg. Check for wrinkles and mold cotton to leg. We use Kendall cotton because it stretches, molds, and tears.

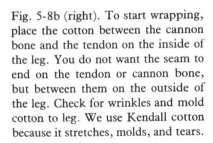

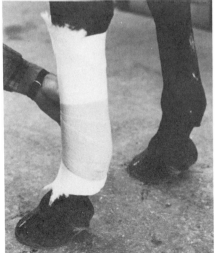

Fig. 5-8c (left). Wrap an Ace bandage around the cotton, starting in the middle of the leg and working down for three or four circuits, then up. Every time you come around to the front, pull a little against the cannon bone. There should be even pressure all the way around.

Fig. 5-8d (left). Secure the bandage with crossed safety pins (or elastic tape).

Fig. 5-8e (right). If you are using the bandages under splint boots for extra support, use elastic tape, but be sure not to pull it too tight. This is a good example of a rundown bandage worn under splint boots for added support.

Poultice bandage (Figure 5.9). Bandage with a poultice used to draw inflammation and heat from the leg. It is an effective treatment for a hot tendon or one that is in danger of bowing. A medicated poultice will draw swelling and heat out of the blood capillaries in the tendon. An anti-inflammatory poultice such as Uptite will reduce swelling and tighten the suspensory ligaments. You can also use a drawing poultice on a foot to clear up infections or for abscesses and stone bruises. A poultice bandage can be applied to any area, and is covered with one or two flannel bandages.

Foot poultice bandage. Used to treat a stone bruise or abscess, to draw out heat and swelling. First, cut the bottom third off a grain bag; then cut it in half to create an oval-shaped envelope out of it. Take Ichthammol or pine tar, apply it to cotton, and pack the foot and smear the pine tar around the heel of the foot. Slip the foot into the corner of the feed bag. Tie up ends. Make ankle straps around the feed bag and hoof, and secure them with a strip of tape. Or, you can wrap the foot with Vet Wrap. This bandage must hold up well and not tear up in the stall overnight.

Poultice bandages should usually be changed every day and a half, although some horsemen leave them on three to four days depending upon the injury. Don't turn out a horse with a poultice or medicinal bandage.

Fig. 5-9a (left). Applying a poultice to the tendon area (Evan Davidson appears here): Start with a bucket of hot water (to wet your hands with) and your chosen poultice. Make sure your horse's leg is clean and dry and the hair is smoothed down.

Fig. 5-9b (right). Wet your hands and scoop out a handful of poultice. Apply it almost like plaster, in thick patches starting just below the knee or at the ankle, building it up and keeping the amount consistent— about an inch thick.

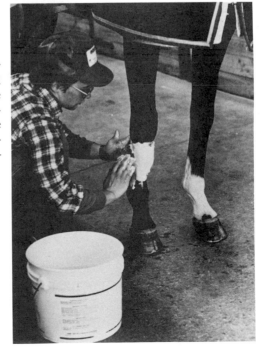

Fig. 5-9c (right). The trick, as with dough, is not to try to work with too much. Keep wetting your hands and applying poultice until it has reached the pastern joint, or just below the knee. Use wet hands to smooth it out—just like a plaster cast.

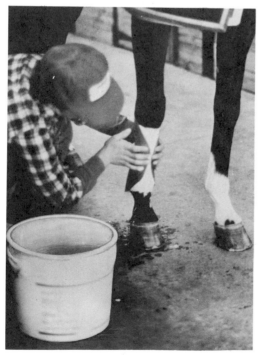

Fig. 5-9d (left). After applying the poultice, take an oval of heavy brown paper, cut from a feed or grocery bag, that has been soaking in hot water, and wrap it around the leg like a splint boot. Paper contains wood pulp, a derivative of DMSO (dimethyl sulfoxide)—a chemical agent that carries medicine through tissue. (An alternative is plastic wrap, which builds up heat inside the bandage, drawing out infection.) Next, wrap leg in flannel bandages.

Sweat bandage. Used to treat splints, osselets, or any similar bone, calcium, or joint inflammations—once cooled down—that produce fibrous tissue buildup causing enlargement of the area and loss of mobility. The heat generated by this bandage will actually sweat out the stiffness, reduce swelling, and bring some suppleness back to the area. There are several types of sweating agents that work well. One is Furacin ointment: Apply a quarter-inch layer of this to the affected area and cover with a single sheet of plastic wrap—just enough to cover the salve. Then apply a standing bandage to cover the sweat and hold in the heat. If you can get one, a U.S. Army bandage—used by medics in the field—works very well. It comes complete with cottons, bandage, and pins, and is very sturdy. Listerine is another excellent sweating agent. It works especially well for reducing soft-tissue problems such as wind puffs and thickened skin from old scars or bucked shins.

Spider bandage (Figure 5.10). Used for sore and swollen knees—a common injury for hunters and jumpers as a result of hitting fences—this bandage covers the knee while allowing freedom of movement.

The spider bandage is complicated, but looks impressive when done right. First, take a piece of flannel sheeting (they come in fourteen-inch squares) and cut approximately twenty half-inch strips, five inches in. Put to one side. Next, wrap the horse's lower leg in a standing bandage, dropping it a little lower than usual over the coronet band. Now, take a brown-paper oval and insert it into the top of the bandage. Fold down. Apply whichever medicated drawing agent you are using (Ichthammol, Furacin, etc.) to the knee. Fold the oval back up over the knee and wrap the leg with six sheet cottons.

Next, take the flannel sheeting cut in strips and wrap it around the leg, covering the knee, with the laces falling to the outside. Braid the laces, crossing over the first two, then dropping them down so that the next two ends cover them. Continue until you've braided all twenty. This technique allows the horse to bend his knee. Don't bind the bandage too tight, or the leg will blow up.

Cold-water bandage. Basically a standing bandage that is kept wet with cold water or an anti-inflammatory solution such as White Lotion, to reduce swelling. It can be created by applying a standing bandage and then hosing the leg (for approximately twenty minutes) to cool it while using support and pressure, or by keeping the bandage on and wetting it periodically throughout the day. (Be careful not to let the bandage dry out, or it will shrink.) In extreme instances ice is sometimes applied directly to the leg and held in place with a bandage. This might happen at a show, or at the onset of an injury to keep it from intensifying.

Fig. 5-10a (right). For the spider bandage, wrap horse's leg in standing bandage and insert brown paper oval. Assemble drawing agents, tape, scissors, and flannel sheeting cut in strips.

Fig. 5-10b (left). Take six sheet cottons and fold them around leg.

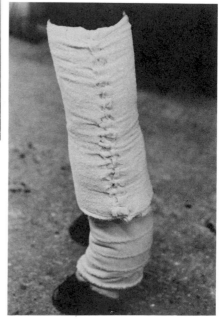

Fig. 5-10c (right). The finished bandage after the flannel sheeting strips have been braided down the leg

Blanketing: The Secret of Layers and Weight

Believe it or not, blanketing a horse properly is a serious concern of the show horse owner, and should not be attempted by the inexperienced. You don't just throw a blanket on a horse come the first signs of cold weather and expect the coat not to grow, and the horse to be comfortable and stay healthy. You know what it feels like to sleep in a hot room with too many bedclothes. That's exactly how a horse feels if you haven't regulated the amount of blanketing to suit the weather and his coat condition. Too much heat can be dangerous and can lead to health problems. A horse can sweat under heavy blankets and catch a chill, get colic, or even build up so much heat that it rushes to his feet and begins to founder him.

The reason we blanket is to stimulate the oils in a horse's coat and to stunt hair growth. Blanketing will also make whatever hair has grown in lie flat. Some horses will keep such a beautiful coat they will not have to be clipped for the indoor circuit in October. Others will have grown enough hair to make us start with a body clip and a hot oil bath before using systematic blanketing.

We do not, as some people do, use a single quilted blanket with a hood. These keep horses warm, but air circulation makes the hair stand up and sometimes grow. Instead, we believe in layers and weight to retain

Fig. 5-11. Wool dress cooler

body oils and stunt hair growth. Sometimes we add and subtract layers during the night (at the 11 P.M. barn check) as the weather cools or warms up. Our students are provided with a wardrobe of blankets (see Table 5.1, Blanketing), most custom-made for perfect fit and to give a uniform appearance to our horses at a show. If you are going to layer, it helps if you are familiar with your barn temperature during the night.

One thing you must always do is make sure your horse is dry and groomed under his blanket. And you also have to be alert for blanket rubs. If you find a blanket chafing the horse—common locations for this are the withers and across the chest—you should sew a protective covering, such as a baby pad or cotton flannel, into that area of the blanket. Keep the rubbed areas moist to help them heal, but be careful about putting Vaseline on damaged hair follicles—white hairs may grow in.

We'll take our horses through the seasons, showing what blankets we use and when we introduce them.

In the summer, we rarely use blankets at all, unless we are at a show where drafty stalls create a wind that can start hair growth. *A horse can begin to grow a coat in one day.* Older horses grow coats quickest. We have one horse that has such a fine coat he is blanketed with a sheet even in the summer months.

But, traditionally, blankets are first put on at night at the Hampton Classic in late August. By mid September, all the horses are wearing at least a sheet at night, sometimes with a blanket over it. During the day they also wear a New Zealand rug when they are turned out, if the weather is cool or breezy. A New Zealand rug (Figure 5.12) is made of durable, stain-resistant material that can take a roll and wet weather to some degree. It has a front buckle, straps around the hind legs, and a front closing. This allows the horse to roll without getting caught up in the blanket or having the blanket slip underneath him—dangers when turning a horse out in a regular blanket.

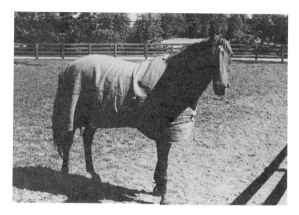

Fig. 5-12. New Zealand rug

TABLE 5.1
BLANKETING

Type	Description	Purpose	Season
Anti-sweat sheet or thermal	Loose, string-knit heavy cotton blanket.	Light protection for warmth to cut down chill. Acts either as a thermal, with holes trapping heat if used in conjunction with other blankets, or as an anti-sweat sheet, with holes letting heat escape so horse doesn't get too hot when used alone. Used under stable blanket, keeps horse from breaking out in a sweat by letting air circulate between blanket and horse.	Spring through fall: alone Winter: with other blankets
New Zealand rug	Stain- and water-resistant cotton/nylon canvas with 5-inch surcingle and straps that fit around back legs.	Allows the horse to be turned out in cooler weather. He can roll and move freely without danger of rug slipping.	Fall through spring
Rain sheet	Made of rain-repellent Cordura nylon, with Velcro closing at neck. Custom-made versions cover head and body.	Worn anytime a horse must go out in inclement weather, with or without tack. Should not be used to cool a horse out with, as material doesn't breathe.	Rain or snow

TABLE 5.1
BLANKETING
(*Continued*)

Type	Description	Purpose	Season
Scrim or fly sheet	Lightest-weight cover, usually a woven fabric. Available in 100% cotton, polyester, or cotton/poly blend. Cotton preferable because it breathes. It does shrink, so order larger size.	To keep dust and insects off horse and tack. Worn up to ring over tack or without as fly sheet.	Warm weather summer
Stable blanket	Available in stain-resistant fabrics with insulating fabric or padding on the inside. Made of 3 layers: outer cover; insulation; fleece, wool, or nylon lining. Has 2 front closings, 2 belly surcingles, tail cord.	Can be used alone or on top of other blankets for extra weight and warmth. Tail cord keeps blanket from slipping. Must fit well—if neck area is too big, blanket will slip back and cause shoulder/chest rubs. To remedy, take up back seam, and make a scoop in fabric and buckles to alter blanket.	Cold weather
Stable sheet	Cotton or cotton/poly blend sheet with 2 front buckles and 2 surcingles front and back.	Worn in the stable, much as a sweater is worn, for warmth. Used as bottom layer when adding thermals, wool liners, and stable blankets.	As the temperature changes

Type	Description	Purpose	Season
Wool cooler	A lightweight wool-blend square with browband, tail cord, and 3 front ties.	Used to take horse to ring in cooler weather. Worn with stable blanket over it for warmth after bath or exercise in cold weather. Anytime you want to cool out a horse in cold weather—protects from wind and chill.	Fall through winter
Wool liner	Heavy wool melton (coating) material with front leather buckle.	Used mainly between cotton sheet and stable blanket for layered warmth. Often added as the night gets cooler in the late fall and early spring.	Fall through early spring

In addition to the preceding wardrobe of blankets, many horses stabled at a particular barn, such as ours, will also have a scrim, wool dress sheet, and thermal with the stable colors and insignia for a uniform appearance ringside.

Fig. 5-13. Stable blanket

During the night throughout the autumn, the layers and weight of the blankets change with the time and temperature. We start with a sheet, move on to a blanket and then to a sheet with a blanket. We watch to see that the horse isn't getting either too hot or too cool. We may crack the barn door or remove or add a blanket as the night progresses.

A horse needs an enormous amount of air to function with maximum efficiency. This means that a stable should have air circulating constantly. Cold air is more beneficial because it holds more moisture—as people with humidifiers already know. You must find a perfect mean between air and body temperature, and proper blanketing will go a long way toward keeping a horse warm and healthy.

As the weather turns colder, we add a wool liner between the sheet and the stall blanket. We never use a thermal overnight, because a horse can catch his feet in the holes. If it is really cold and drafty, we may add two blankets on top of a wool liner, especially for horses that have been body-clipped.

We begin to reverse this process when we ship the horses to Florida in December. They wear a sheet on the way down in the van and in Florida, they wear sheets at night if needed, and coolers or fly sheets during the day to protect them from insects (Figure 5.14). One of the main reasons for blanketing in Florida is to keep the insects from terrorizing the horses. However, the temperature can drop down to 30 degrees overnight, so we have to be alert to changes in temperature, as well.

Fig. 5-14. Scrim or fly sheet (left) and thermal or anti-sweat blanket (right)

Fig. 5-15. Rain sheet

A crucial test of blanketing comes on the return trip in April as we drive from tropical weather into typical spring weather up north. The horses cannot grow coats—we will not body-clip them again until October for the indoor shows. We have to be extra cautious about providing layers of blankets, monitoring the horses until June and the summer circuit is all over. Body-clipping has taken away the horse's natural insulation, and he needs blanketing for warmth as well.

If your horse's coat gets away from you and you see it has started to grow, if you catch it quickly enough you can blanket it and get it to lie down and sleek out. If you have waited too long, you must resort to clipping.

6

Special Effects

The Europeans love to see our braiding, and appreciate our system of yarns.

Bernie LaRocque
braider

Braiding

Braiding manes and tails is the special domain of our master braider Bernie LaRocque, of Southern Pines, North Carolina, shown in Figure 6.1. Originally from Canada, and one of the most respected professional braiders in the field, Bernie cuts a familiar figure on the horse show circuit. Decked out with his apron of colored yarns, his clothespins and braiding needles, Bernie works the thankless hours from midnight to eight in the morning, sometimes braiding upward of twenty manes and tails with his team of four assistants. It takes approximately forty-five minutes to braid a mane and tail. Bernie does all the tails, as they are harder, as well as his share of the more difficult manes.

Because braiding is so hard on the manes and tails, we try to braid as close to a class as possible, and we pull out the braids immediately after the class. If you have ever seen a salt-and-pepper black tail at a horse show, it was probably caused by hairs breaking off or being pulled out by braiding or improper combing. When a hair is pulled out at the roots, nine times out of ten it will grow in white, if you are lucky enough to have it grow in at all. To spare the horses' tails, we seldom braid them for small shows, just the big ones.

Tradition dictates many of the fashions in braiding. Horses' manes were braided for the hunt field in England, so that a rider's hands and whip stayed out of the flying mane, and for neatness and elegance of

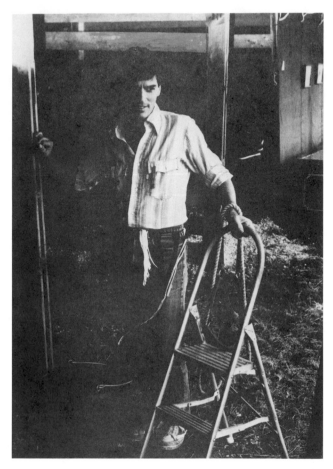

Fig. 6-1. Master braider Bernie LaRocque of Southern Pines, North Carolina, decked out with his tools of the trade

appearance. This practice was translated to the show ring here. The braids were sewn in for stability. In England, mares were traditionally braided with seven braids, geldings and stallions with nine, plus the forelock. Fashions have changed in the past few decades, and today a tastefully braided mane will usually have twenty-two to thirty braids, depending upon the length and shape of the neck and the quality of the mane itself. The braids shouldn't touch or be too far apart or too thick. You can use braids to help camouflage faults and flatter a horse's neck. But the most important thing is that they be strong and consistent. They must stay in and look neat and well matched through schooling, stall rubbing, and a hunter or jumper class.

In the jumper ring today, the favored style is to leave the mane loose and flying free. It adds drama to the motion. Sometimes, though, scalloped braids—long French braids tied together—are put in (see pages 80–81). These are preferred over regular braids because jumper manes are kept longer and if pulled up in the usual way become unattractive sausage-shaped braids.

As with everything else, we have a rigid set of rules about what styles and techniques we accept when it comes to braiding. We want only navy or black yarn used. We don't like to see colored yarns on a hunt course. Bernie uses natural mane colors, such as white for a gray horse, for the yarns that are supposed to be unseen. To keep up our standards of appearance, we braid our horses' manes even for one-day shows.

Fig. 6-2. Kenmere Farm's Lion in Winter. This is a good example of classic hunter braiding.

Equipment

To braid, you will need the following:

2 Afro combs, for combing the tail
2 pairs of scissors, one blunt nosed
2 clothespins, for holding part of mane not being braided
#10 clipper blades, for quick trims of the mane
Seam rippers, to take out braids as soon as a class is over
Needles—rug hooks are recommended—Bernie reshapes his to form
    an oval loop. The commercial ones come with a much wider loop
    that tends to disturb the braids when you pull them through.
Yarns—your stable colors, navy, black, and natural colors for hidden
    yarns
Stool or stepladder
Good lighting or spotlight

Safety Precautions

Most braiding at a horse show is done in the grooming stall or with the horse on cross ties. Tails are often done in the stall with the horse either tied or left loose, depending on how well mannered he is. Our show horses are so used to braiding that they know exactly what we're doing and usually just stand there. Start braiding a horse's mane first, not his forelock, especially if he is unfamiliar to you. If you go quickly to the tail or head, the horse may get nervous. He can see you, and get used to what's happening, if you're at his side. Be careful not to catch the horse off guard when you approach his head or tail. Keep close to him. You will be working in snug quarters, and the closer you are, the less power there is to his kick. Watch for tail swishing. It pulls out braids, but more important, it can hit you in the face and hurt you.

Preparing the Mane and Tail

A mane should be long enough that when it is left unbraided its weight will keep it lying down (Figure 6.3). The usual length is about six inches. If your horse has a heavy crest or a thin neck, you may want to let

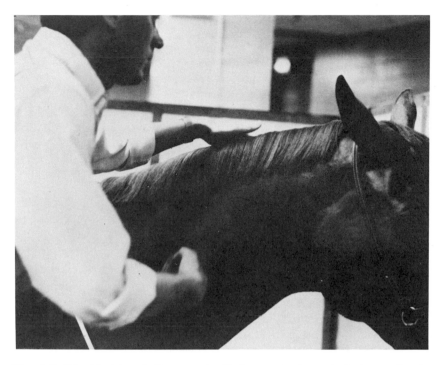

Fig. 6-3. The ideal length for an unbraided mane is about six inches so that it will have enough weight to lie down flat. You may want to taper your mane so that it is shorter at the wither in order to emphasize a long elegant neck or depth of shoulder.

the mane grow longer (heavy crest) or shorter (thin neck), so that when you braid it the braids will compensate for the problem. You want your mane to look good unbraided. A mane should be pulled by an experienced groom or braider about once a month.

A good way to train the mane to lie flat is to wet it with a sponge (Figure 6.4) or water brush before exercise or work and when the horse is put up for the night, or to drape a hot, wet towel over it after the horse has been bathed (Figure 6.4). This also makes for a neater appearance when you tack the horse for lessons and exercise. Some people put in approximately six to eight training braids to help a coarse, thick mane lie flat. Training braids are basically just thick, loose braids, fastened with rubber bands. We don't use them because our horses' manes are braided so often that this could be damaging.

A horse's mane and tail must be clean. Cleanliness helps to promote growth and keeps snarls and tangles to a minimum. We don't suggest you bathe them as often as the horse; sometimes it is necessary to wash them separately. Always use a mild soap, and don't shampoo the day you braid.

Fig. 6-4. Wet the mane with a damp sponge (or water brush) to help train it to lie flat. To save the horses' manes we don't use training braids.

Bernie also asks us not to use a cream rinse to remove tangles the day before he braids because it makes the hair too soft to hold them.

Pure lanolin promotes hair growth, but applying it is a messy business. We use it only on the tail. Smear lanolin into the tail and leave it in— don't wash it out. You will see the results sometime between a week and a month later. The ideal time for revitalizing a tail is when you are laying up your horse—say, in December.

Pulling the Mane

In order to keep the mane growing even and full, it is necessary to pull it regularly. Pulling a mane is exactly what it sounds like: The longer hairs are pulled out by the roots, leaving the shorter, even hairs. Removing the longer hairs not only evens the mane but thins it slightly so that it will lie down flat at the crest. We pull manes as needed, and in between sessions we may snip off stray long hairs with a #10 clipper blade used as a razor (Figure 6.5).

The mane must be clean and combed before it can be pulled. Grab the longer hairs with your fingers and hold them taut. Push the remaining hairs up to the crest with an Afro comb. Pull the remaining longer hairs out at the roots (Figure 6.6). Back-combing the short hairs and then wrapping the longer ones around a comb and tearing them out is the wrong way to pull a mane. You end up with broken hairs, and the mane tends to fly away and stand up straight at the crest.

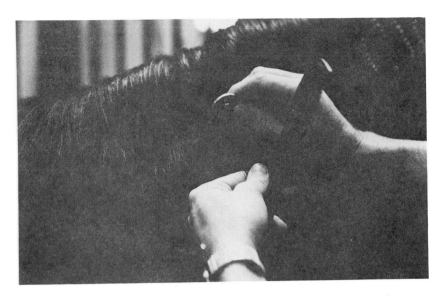

Fig. 6-5 (above). You may need to trim unwanted longer hairs in the mane rather than pull them out. Hold long hair firmly and snip off with #10 clipper blades.

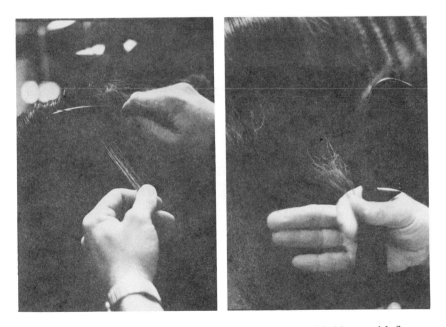

Fig. 6-6a (left). To pull the mane, grab the longer hairs and hold taut with fingers, while pushing the shorter hairs up to the crest with an Afro comb.

Fig. 6-6b (right). Pull the long hairs out by the roots.

Shaping the mane is very important; it can do a lot to flatter a horse's head and neck lines. We like a mane that tapers toward the wither. That way, the throatlatch appears narrower and the shoulder deeper. If you taper your horse's mane so that it is longer at the withers, his neck will appear shorter.

The Forelock

First wet the forelock with a wet sponge. This helps braids stick together and lock tighter. Take three strands of hair, one from each side, and cross them under rather than over as in regular braids. Take the strands into one hand, leaving a free hand to gather hair. Lay a strand of yarn (the same color as the mane) into the V formed by the crossing strands. This yarn will disappear, and incorporating it into the braid will give you extra stability. This works especially well if you have shorter hairs at the poll. Don't braid by pulling away from the crest; keep your hands as close to it as possible. You are forming a French braid, with the ridge appearing on the top of the braid. This braid looks neat and will lock in the shorter hairs.

Don't braid the forelock all the way down. The braid should extend only about three inches when it is pulled through unless your horse has a long head. Then, take your pull-through needle and insert it at the top of the braid at the crest and push it through slowly. Insert the hair that has not been braided through the needle and pull up so that the hair of the pigtail disappears behind the braid (Figure 6.7).

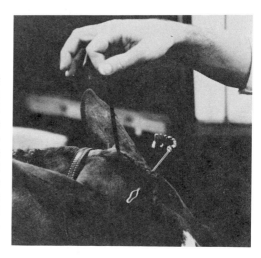

Fig. 6-7. After braiding the forelock, insert pull-through needle behind braid from poll and thread yarn. Pull needle back up and the unbraided pigtail will disappear behind the braid. Then insert a threaded needle across the bottom of the braid about a half inch from the end. Pull threads across and knot to add stability and foreshorten a horse's forehead.

Now, just the ridge will be showing along the length of the forelock. For stability, insert the needle across the braid at the bottom and thread with yarn, double-tie the yarn with a square knot, and cut the end off flush with the braid. We always use navy or black yarn when it will show in the braid. If you need to use additional yarn to bind loose hairs, use a natural color. *Don't* cut these hairs. Horses need every hair we can spare.

You can design the braid to flatter or detract from the horse's conformation. If you put the cross yarns at the very top of the forelock, the head will look longer. If you tie them farther down, say half an inch to an inch, the head will look shorter. A top yarn will also keep loose stubble from tickling a horse's ears.

The Mane

If your horse is wearing a blanket, be sure to undo the front fastening and the surcingles and pull the blanket back so that you can braid to the wither.

Wet the mane with a sponge. Now, section off the piece of hair you will be braiding. Clip the rest out of the way with a clothespin. Mane braids are exactly the same kind as women put in their hair. Braid toward you, incorporating yarn at the bottom of the braid. We don't use rubber bands, except for training braids. The English sew in braids for stability; they braid the night before a hunt, and leave the horses braided overnight. These braids, called "button" braids, are extremely tough to pull out when sewn. They are round and very sturdy, but not as pleasing or graceful to look at as the ones we put in for the show ring in the United States.

Don't braid all the way to the end of the hair. Mane hairs differ in length and type, and this allows you to end up with braids of a consistent length. Braid to exactly the same point on each braid, no matter how long the pigtail is. About half an inch before you end your braid, incorporate a piece of yarn into the braid. Using yarn to tie up braids makes them lie flat—you can't get that effect with the button braid. The finished braid should be between two and two and one half inches long.

Now, insert a needle behind the braid at the crest and push it down the length of the braid. Thread the yarn in the needle and then pull the needle back up toward the crest and all the way through the top of the braid so that the yarn is now lying on the other side of the mane. Pull on the yarn until the braid makes a loop and the unbraided part disappears into the hair at the crest. Pull the yarn over the crest and under the braid, and double-knot it as close to the crest as possible (Figure 6.8). Now pull

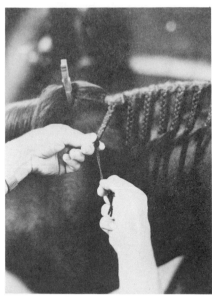

Fig. 6-8a (right). To tie off a braid, incorporate yarn about one half inch before you finish braiding.

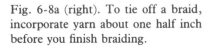

Fig. 6-8b (left). Insert the pull-through needle at the crest and push through behind the braid, making certain it passes through the center.

Fig. 6-8c (right). Thread yarn and pull needle back up so that the yarn lies on the other side of the horse's neck.

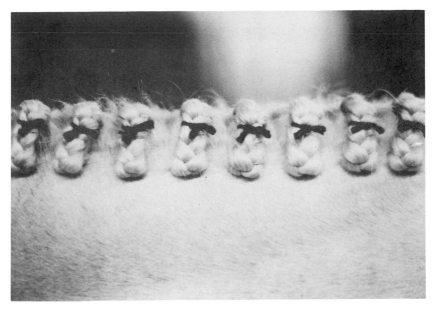

Fig. 6-9. Braids should be uniform, not touching and not too fat, and should lie flat.

the yarn tighter at the top of the braid and this will create a little bubble in the braid. Push the bubble with your thumb so that it breaks. The braid will then lie flat (Figure 6.9). Tie off the yarn with three double loops.

Continue braiding down the neck, planning from twenty-two to thirty braids. (Expert braiders such as Bernie can judge the number of braids just by looking at the mane, but many people section it off before starting.) Bernie always does half of the mane at a time—leaving the last braid in the first half untied so as not to disturb any finished braids—in order to keep the length and shape of the braids consistent. The braids should be uniform, not touching, and not too fat. Lots of braids on the neck will give you the elegant effect you want in the hunter ring.

Jumper Classes

Many riders today prefer the look of a free-flowing mane in jumper classes. If a horse's mane is braided, the most popular style is the scalloped look (Figure 6.10).

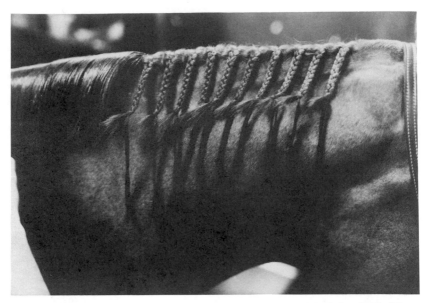

Fig. 6-10a. Scalloped braids: First braid the mane as usual, doing half of it at a time.

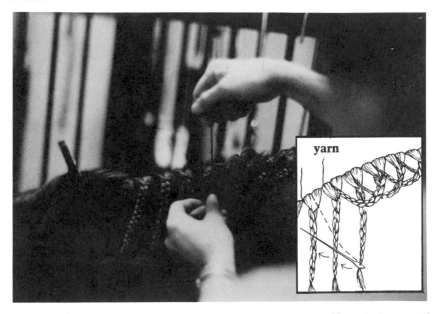

Fig. 6-10b. Thread the pull-through needle as usual, with yarn from the bottom of the first braid, but insert needle at the crest behind the *third* braid, skipping the second. Then go back and pull yarn from the second braid through behind the fourth braid, and so on. The scalloped effect is achieved by skipping every other braid down the neck (see insert).

Fig. 6-10c. Bring the yarn back over the crest and under the braid, tie with a double loop for security, and snip off each piece of yarn at the knot.

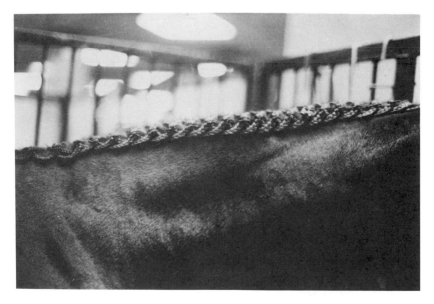

Fig. 6-10d. The full effect—a sleek neck of scalloped braids. This particular job was done on Corsair, at Madison Square Garden, for Olympic Grand Prix rider Leslie Burr.

The Tail

First, get the tangles out of the tail. Use an Afro comb and your fingers. When you hit a snag with the comb, don't tear the hair by forcing the comb through. Use your fingers to pull and separate the knots strand by strand.

When you are ready to braid, start by wetting the tail with plain water, so the hairs will adhere and make a firm braid. This is a trick we use for stability and to catch up broken hairs at the top of the tail where the braid so easily comes undone. Be sure you start with a fair amount of hair; it compresses as you braid. Too much hair will look unnatural and won't hold as well. Take a strand of yarn and lay it straight down the tail from the top and incorporate it into the first folded-in strand of the braid (Figure 6.11). When you cross your first strand again, lay in a second piece of yarn and then a third for the third crossover. For each strand of braid, you will have three pieces of yarn, which will add strength and stability.

Braid so that the ridge forms on the underside. Stop braiding when you have about four inches of unbraided hair strands—the pigtail—just above the tailbone (Figure 6.12). The flowing, unbraided part of the tail is the switch. A long one improves the proportions and appearance of the horse.

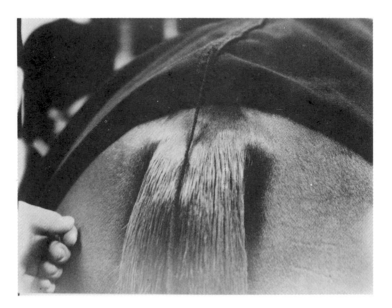

Fig. 6-11. Take a strand of yarn and lay it straight down the center of the tail before crossing over the first strand of the braid.

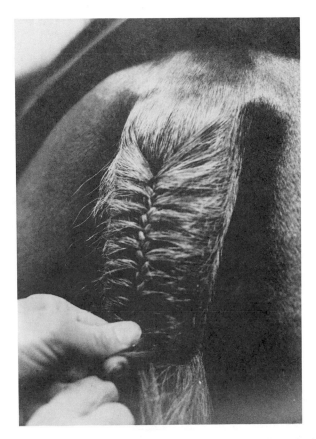

Fig. 6-12. Braid with the ridge forming on the underside. Stop braiding about four inches from the end of the tailbone.

Now, tuck your pull-through needle into the tail hair close to the tailbone and push through to the end of the braid. Thread the yarn and pull the needle up. This will draw the pigtail under the braided tail so that it disappears. Now, insert the needle threaded with rug yarn crosswise down the tail at intervals—three or four times—and thread yarn and pull through. Tie a square knot and cut the yarn right at the knot. This is for stability, to help hold the tail in and bind up loose hairs (Figure 6.13).

You can encounter all kinds of problems when doing tails, such as finding no hair on one side of the tail. At a show you have to learn how to cope with rubbed-off patches of mane and rubbed tailbones or missing hairs, all of which make for difficult braiding. A trick one braider used was to braid a long pigtail on one side of a tail with no hair on the opposite side. He then wrapped this braid around the tail as artfully as possible so that it would look braided at a distance.

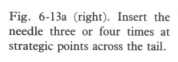

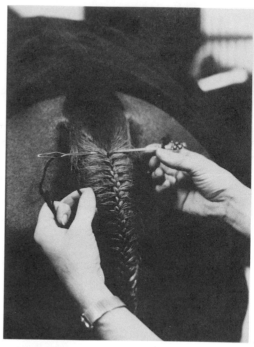

Fig. 6-13a (right). Insert the needle three or four times at strategic points across the tail.

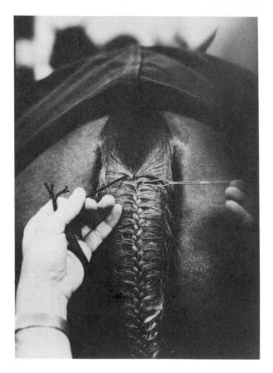

Fig. 6-13b (left). Thread and pull through. Tie yarn with a square knot and clip close.

Tail Wraps

As soon as a horse's tail is braided, apply a tail wrap so that the braid cannot be rubbed off in the stall while he waits for his class. It is also used during shipping for a horse that rubs in the van. The best material for a tail wrap is an Ace bandage.

First, wet the tail wrap. A wet tail wrap sticks to the braid so that any little wispy hairs will lie flat when it is removed. Also, the wrap won't slide down if it has been slightly dampened.

Start the bandage at the top, right under the tailbone, and wrap to the bottom of the braid, then wrap back up to the middle. Take your thumb and pull out a fold of the bandage, slip the remaining end of it in and release your thumb. Remove the tail wrap *just before* you enter the ring to show.

The Mud Knot

A mud knot is a knot tied with the switch of the tail. There are several reasons for using one, and several varieties.

To get the tail out of the way for barn chores, and when a horse is being bandaged or worked on, you can simply grab his tail, twist it around

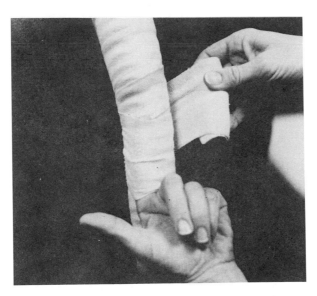

Fig. 6-14. To tuck in bandage, take your thumb and pull bandage outward. Slip the end of the bandage into the pocket created, and release. Never cover a pinwheel.

as you would a ponytail, and tie it in a loop. For schooling or showing in mud, braid the tail as usual, then take the remaining switch and split it in half. Bind one half around behind the dock of the tail; do the same with the other. Crisscross the two halves as you wrap them around the dock of the tail, binding one over the other, then tie the hair up.

The mud knot is sometimes also used to show off a hunter with a good hindquarter.

Pinwheels: A Very Special Effect

This artful way to finish off a tail is currently popular on the hunter circuit, and Bernie is a master at it. To make a pinwheel, continue braiding the pigtail about eight inches past the end of the tailbone. Incorporate yarns as you would for regular tail braiding, and tie a double knot at the bottom for security. Leave yarns trailing. Now you are ready to roll the pinwheel. Don't fold the end of the pigtail and place it at the end of the tailbone so that it just lies flat or the pinwheel will not be rounded, and will stick out strangely. Instead, make sure that the top of the folded pigtail is shorter than the bottom so that you have a crescent effect. Then continue to roll the pigtail up the tailbone—you will end up with a symmetrical, circular pinwheel (Diagram 6.1). Once you have rolled up the pinwheel, run your needle through the center of it. Catch the yarns and then pull back through the center. Tie off with one regular knot and one square knot for security (Figure 6.15).

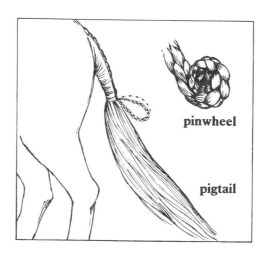

Diagram 6-1. Rolling the pinwheel

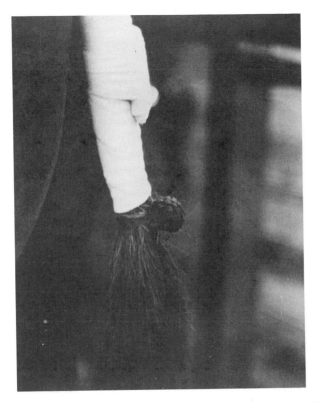

Fig. 6-15. Braided tail with a pinwheel protected by wrap before class. We usually put pinwheels in for all the big shows.

Pulling

Many people don't braid their horses' tails but pull them and bang them instead. Banging consists of a blunt cut straight across at the hocks. In the hunter show world we don't trim tails, unless it is a very subtle snipping to promote growth and for appearance when loose, but it is a grooming technique you should know about.

To pull a tail you pluck out the hairs along the sides of the tail, high up on the bone, with pliers. With the hairs along the sides removed, when the unbraided tail arches away from the body, little hairs won't drop down and destroy the line.

The braids we have illustrated for you in this chapter are the ones we find acceptable, tasteful, and stylish for the hunter and jumper rings—our main concern. Although there are other variations, we stick closely to these.

Trimming

Trimming a hunter or jumper is a very exacting job, and the procedure is basically the same for every type of horse. You simply remove the hair that grows in where the bridle will rest, snip off unsightly hairs around the face and neck for a sleek elegant head, and trim the tufts of hairs at the fetlock and coronet band. The specific areas that should be trimmed are the muzzle, throatlatch, chin, nose, and the hairs just around the eyes, ears, bridle path, fetlocks, and coronet bands.

Trimming is the grooms' responsibility here. We trim our horses before every show, preferably the day before they ship, or when they need it. Even when we stable a horse that is not being shown regularly or is being let down for some reason, we trim him every few weeks.

Always start with a clean and dry horse. You can't clip a horse that is dirty or wet. Place the horse on cross ties in a good direct light. Use a spotlight if you have to. Always try to have someone on hand to assist you, and make sure you have all the necessary supplies at hand and ready to use.

Fig. 6-16. Clipping essentials for trimming or a full body clip: broom * pail * extension cord * oil for blades * oil for clippers * large body clippers * small clippers * clipper blades * screwdrivers * towel * twitches (humane and chain)

Equipment

To trim, you will need the following:

Small ladder or footstool, to stand on	Lubrication oil for clipper blades
Small animal clippers	Oil for clippers
Set of screwdrivers to adjust blades	Extension cord
#40 clipper blades	Towel
Soft brush	Humane twitch (see Restraints on pages 106–107)
Hard brush	Broom

Before you begin to trim a horse, turn on the clippers and allow him to get used to the sound and vibration. While they are running, place them near his nose and muzzle to get his confidence (Figure 6.17).

To trim a horse properly, think of yourself as a painter. The key to a successful trimming job is to blend the whiskers and tufts into the rest of the horse's coat so that there is no noticeable difference between them. To achieve this, you should hold the trimming clippers as if they were a paintbrush; firmly, but without gripping. To reach all the hairs—such as the ones under the chin—feel free to use the clippers upside down and backward.

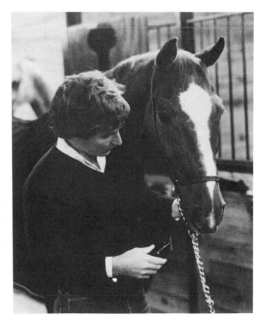

Fig. 6-17a. Before you start to trim, get your horse used to the sound and vibration of the clippers. Turn them on and place them near the muzzle and nose—areas he can see.

Fig. 6-17b (right). Start with the muzzle. Using light pressure, trim the hairs around the muzzle and nostrils.

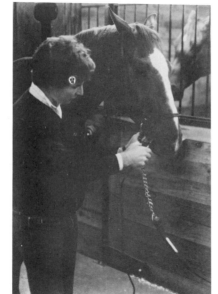

Fig. 6-17c (left). Next do the mouth. Use the most pressure here—it is somewhat like shaving a man's face.

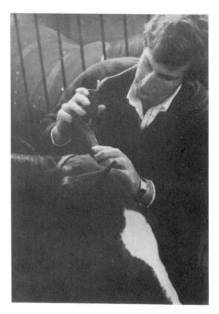

Fig. 6-17d (right). After trimming the bridle path, go on to the ears. Trim the outside of the ears first. Begin at tip and follow outline down.

One way to ensure a good trim is to look at your work from different angles. Some areas will be in the shade. Check both sides. Clip across the horse to the opposite side in each direction to get a better blend of hair. Remember to turn your clippers off occasionally to let them cool. They get hot as you work, and can irritate the nostrils or other sensitive areas.

The Head

Start with the horse's muzzle. Clip against the grain of the hair. Use light pressure and trim the hairs in his nostrils (don't go too far in) and the loose hairs around the muzzle. This is a good place to start because he can see what's happening and the sound is not near his ears. You rarely need a restraint when you're doing this area. Next, clip the hairs around the mouth. This is where you will need the most pressure. It is like shaving a man's face. You can use your fingers to stretch out the wrinkles around the mouth. You should always smooth out wrinkles as you trim, so that the clippers will cut evenly and thoroughly.

Sometimes scraggly hairs begin to grow in under the chin or at the throatlatch. This happens partly because the horse's blanket doesn't usually cover this area. Clip with a blending stroke in the direction the hair lies to nip off these hairs for a quick touch-up.

As you work up the head, the hairs will grow more sparsely, and you may be clipping individual hairs. Be careful not to nick the face, and that the trimmed portions blend into the fine face hairs. Never trim a horse's eyelashes, but do snip the guard hairs under the eyes. These can be trimmed short, but should never be cut off, because if you are turning your horse out, or even when he is in his stall, these feeler hairs protect the horse and alert him when he is in too tight a space and might injure himself.

After doing the muzzle, nose, eyes, and throatlatch, you are ready to trim the bridle path. We like ours two inches wide, enough room for the bridle and halter. To begin, get a stool and place it at the side of the horse. Make sure the clippers' cord is out of the way by keeping it in front of you. Start at the point of the poll. Hold the forelock out of the way and, using light pressure, work your way two inches down the bridle path. You should leave the horse's halter on and simply move it back and forth as you trim. If your horse has too wide a bridle path, allow his mane to grow in until it is gradually reduced to two inches.

The Ears

Now you are ready to trim the ears. Here you must proceed with caution, as horses are ultrasensitive to sound and vibrations around their eardrums. Make sure your horse is used to the sound of the clippers and that they're cool. Investigate his ears before starting to make sure there is no irritation or infection caused by burdocks, gnats, small tumors, or sores. Try to sense whether or not your horse is going to be head shy. If you have his confidence—begin. If not, you'll need to apply a twitch. We use a humane twitch and prefer to have someone hold it. If you don't have an assistant, clip the twitch onto the horse's halter.

Trim the outer edge of the ears first and work inward. Hold the ear with your free hand, using your fingers to press the inside flap of the ear out. Begin at the tip and follow the outline down. Make the first cut with the back of your blades, not the edge. Make sure the clippers are cutting properly, with the blades sharp and not loosened, and are not too hot. Try to have a second pair on hand, so you can change clippers when you have to cool one of them.

After trimming the outside of the ear, fold it inside out from the bottom to trim the inside. Use light strokes, being careful not to gouge your horse with the clipper blades as you trim crevices.

The Fetlocks and Coronet Bands

The last areas to be trimmed are the fetlocks and coronet bands, where tufts of hair grow at the ankle. You have to be very careful to blend these hairs in with the leg. Again, think of the clippers as a paintbrush, and cut across the hair in a straight line, not against it at an angle.

Finishing Up

When you are finished, brush and towel off your horse and double-check your work. A trim should take ten to fifteen minutes, tops.

Clipping

The Full Body Clip

Doing a full body clip takes practice, and through the years we have devised a system that works for us. It is a time-consuming process that takes about two to three hours. The ideal way to get maximum results from a body clip is to keep your horse's coat beautifully maintained. If his coat is in good condition and has been properly maintained all year long, you will lose very little color or coat condition with one body clip, but if you clip a second time too soon, the coat will lose a substantial amount of color and richness. (Gray horses can be clipped more often.) We usually clip at least twice a year—once before the fall indoor shows at Harrisburg, Washington, D.C., and New York, and a second time when we get to Florida in January.

Equipment

To do a full body clip you will need the following:

Broom
Stepladder or footstool
Towels
Extension cord
2 large animal clippers
Lubrication oil for blades
Screwdrivers to adjust blades
Electric clipper grease
Body-clipping blades, size #slo5 and #0104
Half-and-half mixture of kerosene and motor oil (in bucket or large
    can)
Small animal clippers, for trimming
Humane twitch and chain twitch (see Restraints, pp. 106–107, 108)
Hard brush, for brushing off horse before you clip
Soft brush, for brushing clipped areas
Long-sleeved nylon windbreaker, to protect you from loose hair
Handkerchief or tissue, for wiping away loose hair from nose and eyes

We use Oster clippers, lubrication oil, and clipper grease.

First, bathe your horse. Before clipping, make sure he is thoroughly dry and that his coat is brushed and lying flat.

Get the horse used to the noise of the clippers; then approach him while they are running. Don't turn them on when you have them against the horse—this may jar and spook him. Clip against the hair except when you are blending.

Start clipping at the shoulder. It helps if you always start to clip an area where the horse can see what's happening and that is not too sensitive to sound and vibration. This way he has an opportunity to accept the clippers, and there's less chance that you'll be injured. Use short, repeated

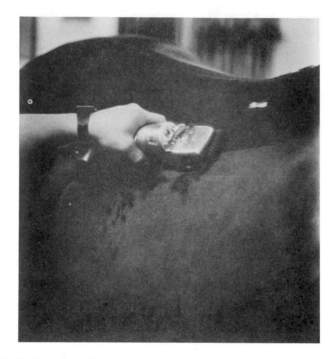

Fig. 6-18. Use broad strokes for back, flanks, stomach, and sides. Repeat strokes over area and "half-track" to cover clipper traces and lines.

strokes, as if you were mowing a lawn; after you've clipped an area, cover half of it with the blade and begin a new one. Then rub the clippers back and forth over the clipped areas to cover trace lines.

After clipping the shoulder, go up to the neck to just behind the cheekbone, close to the head, and just below the crest of the mane.

Next clip the back, flanks, stomach, and sides. Here you can use broader strokes, but continue to track over clipped areas. Clip the front legs to above the knee, then approach the sensitive areas of the girth, lower legs, head, and underbelly. Make sure your blades are not too hot, and keep them oiled, dipping them about every fifteen minutes into a kerosene/oil mixture. You may also have to change blades or adjust them occasionally—as you work, they tend to shift, making them either too tight or too loose. Use screwdrivers to make adjustments.

After you go over an area the first time, brush away remaining hairs so that you keep the job neat and can see what you are working on. For a good clip, the first swipe should be thorough with no nicks. To avoid nicks, use smaller strokes, well-lubricated equipment, and clear light, and start with a healthy, clean coat.

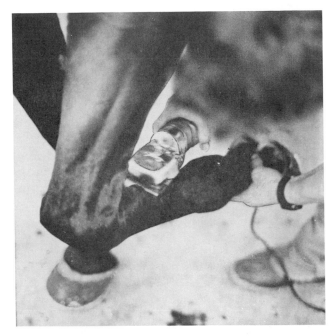

Fig. 6-19. When clipping the legs, don't be afraid of going against the hair, unless you are blending at the fetlocks. Hold the leg up for ease and control while clipping.

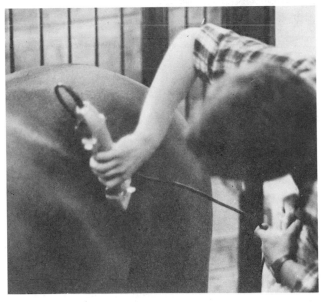

Fig. 6-20. For hard-to-reach crevices, maneuver clippers deftly.

Finishing off the clipping requires some special touches. The proper way to finish around the tailbone is to blend the point of the croup in a V on each side of the bone by turning the clipper blades down. For the mane, be sure to clip both sides as close to the crest as possible. Mane hair is very different from body hair and it really looks strange if any is left. The head and ears are the last areas you clip. You may need to use a twitch at this point. You do not have to change clippers to do this. Trace the head with the clippers and then go back and trim the area around the muzzle, nose, ears, and eyes. Use trimming clippers for the whiskers.

After a body clip, bathe your horse in warm water and baby oil (about half a cup to a bucket of water). The oil will replenish the natural oils lost in the clipping process and soothe tender skin. Then begin a careful

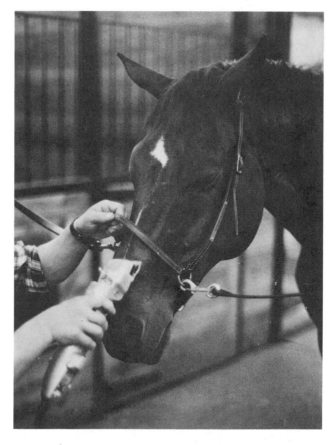

Fig. 6-21. Use the same large clippers for the head as for the body. Skim the horse's head all over, then use trimming clippers on muzzle, nose, eyes, and ears and to clip whiskers.

blanketing and grooming program to try and maintain the coat in good condition and avoid the need for a second clip too soon after the first. There are horror stories, involving even some of the top stables and horse shows, about what can happen to a body clip that is not carefully monitored. At the National Horse Show one year, a top jumper that had been given a body clip three days before was stabled under the ventilating fan. By the fifth day of the show, he had grown a full head of hair! Remember, a horse can begin to grow a coat in one day, and there are several particularly vulnerable areas. As hunter and jumper owners do not usually use hoods to protect their horses' heads, this is one. And watch for hair growth under the stomach or on the sides of the neck, which may not be covered by a blanket. When you put a stable blanket over a long cooler, be sure to pull it up tight around the belly to avoid this.

Leg and Trace Clips

Sometimes a full clipping of the legs, to the shoulder, is necessary, because sufficient hair has grown in before it is time for a full body clip. We always clip the legs, if they need it, at least a week before we ship the horses to Florida, so that by the time we get there the hair will have grown in enough to protect the skin from sand and fungus infections. You can also clip a horse's legs below the knees when the hair starts to grow in, in the spring and fall, to remove "road maps"—bandage lines or marks from pinfiring. In cold months, when the horse's coat has grown in, some owners do a trace clip instead of a full clip. This means clipping areas that will get sweaty from bearing tack, so that the horse can properly cool out and dry. We don't have a need for this type of clip at Beacon Hill.

Shedding

In a show barn we rarely have to deal with this situation. The horses may grow a slight winter coat, but through blanketing, grooming, and clipping, we avoid heavy shedding. However, horses will shed even a medium-thick winter coat; ours begin to shed when they return from Florida and continue through the late-spring shows. If this happens, do what we do—groom, groom, groom. Reach for that curry comb and rub rag and keep rubbing and currying until no more hair comes out. It might take one or two hours a day, for a week or two, to get off a long coat. The curry comb will help the horse shed and the rub rag will draw the natural oils to the surface of the coat and increase circulation—all of which makes for a shiny, light coat. Blanketing will help smooth down the hair that has grown and will speed up the process; every horse at our barn that is let down for the winter is turned out in a New Zealand rug and brushed daily to keep hair growth at a minimum. Bathing will also help remove loose and dead hair and accelerate the shedding, but elbow grease is really the only approach we know to shed out a horse.

7

Problem Solving

Use common sense. Approach an injury or problem with a horse without panic. If you work as a
team with your vet, farrier, trainer, and groom,
you should be able to tackle any problem that
arises.

Joe Heissan, DVM
New England Equine Practice
Ridgefield, Connecticut

Many things can happen to a horse—injuries, skin diseases, eye infections, saddle and blanket rubs—that are common horse care problems not
necessarily involving sickness or disease. The latter should be the exclu-
sive domain of an attending veterinarian.

When these problems arise at a horse show they have to be treated on
the spot. Then, we must rely on the expertise of our barn manager and
grooms, working in tandem with a veterinarian, if possible.

Over the years, we have settled on certain treatments that work for us
on routine problems. We thought it might be helpful to encapsulate these
problem-solving techniques in chart form as a handy guide. We want to
emphasize that these remedies have evolved as a result of many situations
and that you should never use them without first checking with your
veterinarian.

High-Tech Therapy

As horsemen, the future is upon us. We are fast entering the world of
medical high tech, where yesterday's problems are being solved today by
the latest advances in ultrasound and laser technology. Although we still

employ such beneficial healing and preventative agents as bandaging, blistering, and other slower-acting remedies, we must also incorporate the newest, timesaving, less invasive and non-painful forms of therapy available. We feel that a current book on grooming and horse care would not be complete if it did not touch on these advances. Whereas, a few years ago, a horseman's only means of healing a big knee injury incurred while jumping was a spider bandage using a drawing agent such as Ichthammol, today we can turn to these new technologies to promote healing and reduce swelling. We can also deal with chronic pain and bring a horse back to work more quickly through the use of these high-tech therapeutic aids.

The following is a layman's guide to some of the new treatments currently available and their most appropriate and beneficial uses.

Ultrasound. Stimulates healing and increases blood circulation by employing high-frequency sound waves to penetrate soft tissue. The vibrations from the waves cause friction, and therefore heat, in the tissues, thereby increasing circulation, which aids the healing process. Ultrasound is used to break down fibrous tissue in splints, ankles, knees, shoulders, and capped hocks, among other conditions. The advantage of ultrasound over the earlier, more conventional methods of bandaging and blistering is that it does not cause further trauma to the area or invade the skin, and it can produce dramatically quicker results.

Muscle Stimulator. A hand-held, battery-powered machine that is applied to an area to electrically stimulate muscles. Muscle stimulation is an excellent way to exercise the muscles of a horse not kept in work, or one that has suffered nerve damage due to injury until the nerve is repaired, to prevent atrophy of the muscles involved. The muscle stimulator actually sends the same electrical impulses to the muscles that a nerve would, causing them to twitch involuntarily. It is ideal for back problems, bruises, strains, keeping the horse fit, or building up weak muscles.

Laser. Works by creating light amplification by stimulated emission of radiation (hence the name). The laser focuses light in such a way as to stimulate certain tissue components in the area being treated while at the same time increasing the flow of blood to the wound. It promotes healing without disturbing the surface of the skin and—perhaps its most therapeutic advantage—without pain. Used primarily for lower-leg problems such as bowed tendons and injuries to suspensory ligaments, as well as chronic wounds and sores and on surgical incisions and freshly stitched cuts to promote fast healing.

TABLE 7.1

PROBLEM SOLVING ON THE HORSE SHOW CIRCUIT

Blanket rubs: Sew fleece or baby pads into blanket, corresponding to area where rub appears—usually withers, shoulders, or chest. Keep soft with baby oil. Vaseline will produce white hairs if the hair follicles have been damaged.

Capped hocks: Bruised hock which fills with fluid that can harden into calcium deposit. When injury is still new and hot, apply cold water 20 minutes a day, 3 times a day. After hock has cooled, apply DMSO (dimethyl sulfoxide) and Azium mixture. Consult vet.

Cuts: Clean area thoroughly. Don't be afraid to scrub as bleeding helps heal. Cuts, even minor ones, heal more quickly when stitched, and horse can be kept in work. Leave scrubbed and exposed to air to promote healing, or apply antibiotic and pressure bandage, depending on nature of cut. If proud flesh develops, apply medicated agent to erode granulated tissue.

Eyes: Consult vet. Don't treat this yourself with any old eye medication you might happen to have lying around. Many contain steroids, and if there is a tear or ulcer in the eye, they can cause blindness.

Fistula: A wither sore caused by improper saddle padding, dirty pads, and ingrown hairs. Rest horse. Clean area thoroughly and squirt antibiotic ointment deep into sore. Don't allow outside to heal first— keep open until inside has closed up.

Fungus: Captan (a commercial rose fungus spray in powder form that our vet mixes up for us) mixed with warm water and used as a rinse, DeFungit, or Colloidal soap. Wash any grooming supplies, stalls, and equipment that came in contact with fungus, as well as all the horses.

TABLE 7.1

PROBLEM SOLVING ON THE HORSE SHOW CIRCUIT (*Continued*)

Grab or clip to bulb:	Caused by horse interfering. Keep clean and soft with a lanolin-based product such as Corona. Keep wrapped. Have farrier check for reason for interference. Horse may need corrective shoeing.
Hives:	Caused by allergic reactions and changes in feed. Cold-water baths are comforting, but call vet to give steroid injection with antihistamine.
Injection site lumps and insect or horse bites:	Use hot packs and Ichthammol to reduce swelling or draw out infection. Ice may be applied to reduce swelling immediately after bite, once area is cleaned. Massage with alcohol.
Puncture:	May look like a small wound, but is actually a deep hole. Clean thoroughly and flush with peroxide or liquid Furacin. Pack with Ichthammol to draw out infection. Allow to heal from inside out. Can also apply DMSO around puncture to reduce swelling and help carry medicine to wounded tissues. For cosmetic cover-up if horse must be shown, coat with antibacterial spray or salve that blends into skin such as Blu-Kote (gray horse), Ichthammol (black horse), or topical antibacterial powder.
Scars and white hairs:	Use a commercial hair coloring such as any instant coloring foam, applied with sponge, to match horse's coat color.
Scratches:	Small cuts behind heel causing soreness. Scrub clean to bleeding point. Apply mixture of Azium, DMSO, and antibiotic ointment such as Furacin or Panolog. Wrap, if needed, to keep clean in a dusty situation.

Sore backs: Try to avoid by using foam pad under saddle for extra protection. Exercise horse by longeing and working loose to avoid weight of rider on back. Saturate a towel with White Lotion (astringent that, used as a wet pack, breaks down fibrous tissue and relieves soreness) and apply to back to reduce inflammation.

Stains: The bane of owners of gray horses. Carry a spray bottle of alcohol to show ring to scrub out. Use commercial blue rinse for gray hair to get out yellow stains.

Stocking up: Ankles become puffy from being stabled for an extended period, or shipped. Walk the horse or give him about 20 minutes' exercise to reduce swelling. Apply alcohol to legs after walk while swelling is down and blood circulation has increased from workout. A Vetrolin body brace helps to prevent this problem.

Stone bruise: When first encountered, cool with ice and poultice overnight. Apply pine tar and hoof pads to help draw out soreness. Brush turpentine on sole to help harden.

Wind puffs and bog spavins: Call vet—could be a sign of torn tendon or other damaging leg injury. If diagnosed as not serious, apply brace bandage, with astringent, and hose down.

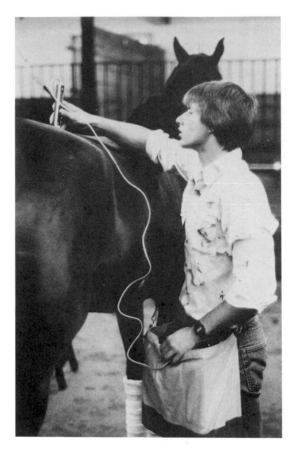

Fig. 7-1. John Ducharme treats a sore back with a Class I laser. Today's barns have come to rely on non-invasive, high-tech forms of therapy.

Lasers are also being used effectively for acupuncture to relieve chronic pain, especially in the back and lower legs (Figure 7.1). Because needles are not inserted into the affected nerves, it is a painless procedure. Laser therapy is very accessible to the horseman and his attending vet. It is available in portable units classed according to potency (e.g., Class 1, Class 3A), and so far it appears unlikely to cause any harmful effects. As the laser is a relatively new therapeutic aid, many of its uses are still experimental.

Electromagnetic Therapy, or as it's known in the horse world, the "blue box," was made famous on the racetrack when it was first used to heal a bone fracture in Conquistador Cielo. His miraculous recovery caused racetrack horsemen to become regular users of this method, which promotes healing through the use of stimulating electrodes that pass an electromagnetic field through the bone. In addition to healing fractures, the "blue box" is used for sore backs, bucked shins, knee chips, and many different sore afflictions. If you travel through a show barn, you will see horses with what appear to be saddle pads on their backs. Electrodes hooked up on each side of the pads and connected to the "box" send electromagnetic waves through the bone and tissue to promote healing and increase circulation through heat. What makes this method popular is its ease. The box is simply plugged in and pads are left on the horse's back, whereas laser or ultrasound machines must be applied manually.

Nebulizer. Another unexpected sight in a show barn, especially one like Madison Square Garden, where the horses are stabled inside and it becomes stuffy and difficult to breathe, is the use of nebulizers. These are vaporizers with masks connected to a hose through which is pumped oxygen mixed with chemicals such as antibiotics or decongestants. The horses wear the masks and inhale this chemical mist, which helps them breathe more easily. For show horses that must perform, this is an excellent, though extreme, remedy for breathing difficulties.

Fig. 7-2. Hydrotherapy is another useful high-tech innovation for reducing inflammation or increasing circulation to treat sore legs and ligament and tendon injuries. The whirlpool can be used with warm or cold water, and with or without air jets, depending on the injury. We use ours in the shower stall, with the horse hand-held or on cross ties.

Restraints

We like to think we handle our horses with approaches in this order:

Ask.
Tell.
Make.

First we *ask* the horse to cooperate when we are approaching a potentially difficult situation such as trimming, loading, or cleaning a sheath. Then, if this isn't enough, we *tell* him by using firm voice commands and handling, making sure we have his attention. Finally, as a last resort, we *make* him submit to whatever he needs to have done by using some form of restraint. We are careful not to put the horse on the defensive right away. We are equally careful not to allow him to get away with being stubborn, or further problems will arise later. Don't forget: By restraining a horse, you are—among other things—trying to prevent him from hurting himself, and you! A good horseman learns to anticipate a problem and be ready for it. Instinct can serve you well.

The following is a list of various restraints and their uses.

Chain lead shank. A common form of restraint that can be used effectively to lead, load, and longe a horse, and get his attention and keep his head down when working on him. Place the chain lead over the noseband of the halter, not under the chin, so that when you tug on the lead shank you can pinch and put pressure on the vulnerable nose (Figure 7.3).

Cross ties. Two ropes, chains, or rubber leads, attached to the rings of the halter on either side of the horse and either hand-held or fixed to walls at the other end. Keeps the horse's head confined and his body straight. May be considered a restraining device. Watch out for the horse pulling back, up, or away in fear or pain. He could lose his footing and injure himself badly—break a wither, for example. Sometimes it is more sensible to use a chain lead shank instead.

Holding up an opposing leg. A way to get a horse to stand still for medication, soaking, or bandaging; also prevents him from striking and kicking.

Chain twitch. A chain loop on a wooden handle. It is more severe than other twitches because the handle allows you to twist it tightly. Try to have someone on hand to hold this type of twitch.

Fig. 7-3. The chain lead shank allows you to control a horse that needs some restraint without using cross ties. You can lace it through the noseband, or simply double-loop it and clip it under the chin as shown here.

Ear twitch. Can be either grabbing the ear with your hand and pulling downward or twisting it, to applying a rope twitch. A good way to control a horse if you are putting in eye medicine, trying to get his head down, or don't have a mechanical twitch handy.

Humane twitch. The one we prefer because it is just that—humane. A nutcracker-like device that grasps the nose and muzzle and then closes tight at the bottom. Useful because it can be held fast with a cord and clipped onto a halter if you don't have anyone to assist you (Figure 7.4).

Rope twitch. A rope looped around the nose and muzzle and held tight. Another way to control or restrain a horse when you don't have a mechanical twitch on hand.

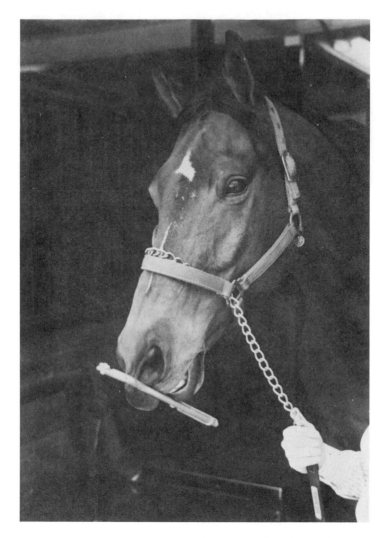

Fig. 7-4. The humane twitch is our preferred restraint.

Shipping

It is all too easy to lose the bloom on a show horse in transit—especially, in our case, during the twenty-two-hour trip to Florida every winter. A lot of accidents can befall a horse while he's being vanned, and a lot of health problems can arise after you unload. We try to avoid these by care and careful planning.

Preparations—Long Distances

For a long trip, such as the one to Florida, we start preparing the horses at least two days before we ship, but we try not to disturb their usual routines. We feed them a bran mash for two consecutive feedings before shipping, and have our vet tube them with oil for protection against intestinal blockage. The horses will have been getting light exercise, and the day before we ship we turn them out. If we are traveling to Florida, their legs will be clipped to the shoulder far enough ahead of time for the hair to have a chance to grow in and protect their skin from irritating sand and fungus. We may also put all of them on a long-lasting (approximately twelve-hour) antibiotic such as procaine penicillin to protect them if one of the horses has a cold, the weather is very bad, or we've heard of an epidemic of shipping fever—a horseman's term for a serious and highly contagious upper respiratory infection horses often get while traveling.

Preparations—Local

Most of our shows are not more than a seven-hour drive away, and many are not more than two or three hours. Even so, we still turn the horses out before they ship, and try not to interrupt their daily routines. Also, it is a good idea to get green or young horses accustomed to shipping, and vanning them to local shows along with seasoned horses is an

Fig. 7-5. The Beacon Hill show van: A 1984, fifteen-horse trailer built by Grand Prix Trailers with air-ride suspension. It is forty-eight feet long and eight and one half feet wide, for maximum room. The tractor is a 1984 White. Two loading ramps with sides make for easy access and loading. The equipment that belongs to grooms and riders is shipped in trunks and saddlebags—all in Beacon Hill colors with insignia—and stored in the roof well.

excellent way to do it. A young or green horse that hasn't been accustomed to vanning can actually lose fifty to one hundred pounds on a long trip.

Vehicle and Staff

Horses will travel only as well as the people you have employed to trailer them. We work with a commercial horse transporter, as do most show barns. They keep our vehicles maintained and have the expertise to handle any problem that may arise. The trailer measures forty-eight feet by eight and one half feet wide. We use two loading ramps with sides, which is the safest way to get a horse on and off a trailer.

On the Road

We often leave early in the morning, but again, we try not to disturb the horses' usual routines. The horses all travel in shipping bandages, sheets or blankets, and tail wraps. They also wear leather halters, with fuzzies (pieces of sheepskin on the straps of the halter) to prevent rubs. Our preference is for stable or standing bandages, with the cottons extended down over the coronet bands and up to the knee. Our cottons are custom-made and extra thick, so that it is almost impossible for a horse to get close enough to another leg to clip himself. Also, to prevent injuries, every horse ships in a double stall. This allows some mobility, prevents crowding, and provides easy access to horses. We make sure lead ropes, chain shanks, and a twitch are readily accessible in case of a problem.

We always travel with our horses on long-distance runs, such as the one to Florida, and the grooms ride in the trailer with them. After four hours on the road, we offer the horses water, and check on bandages, blankets, and their overall condition. We feed only hay on the ride, keeping it in front of the horses at all times. On the way to Florida we lay over in Camden, South Carolina, for a day or two, depending upon weather conditions and the health and attitude of the horses. This is about twelve hours into the trip, or halfway to our destination. When vanning long distances we try to organize the trip to entail no more than twelve hours on the road per day. While we are laying over we check to make sure that the horses are contented and eating well—they get one half their normal feed ration—and have normal temperatures.

Because of this regime, when we arrive after a long trip the horses are not drawn up from lack of water, sore, or dull looking. Horses may need as much as a week to revive if they do not receive proper care in transit. We like to see them come off the trailer fresh and alert. We ship them down to Florida early enough that they can be put back in light work and become gradually conditioned for the show schedule. This means at least a month before the shows start.

8

Tack

Tack can be used to help the horse perform, but it
can also flatter conformation flaws.

Nothing looks better in the show ring than seasoned tack. One of the most
beautiful bridles we own is the one that has been used on the champion
hunter Dillon. It is eight years old, and is attractively worn—the leather
has richness and suppleness. It is classically simple in design and flawlessly
maintained. This is the ideal look for hunter tack.

It is essential that a rider have the right equipment. Tack is first a
rider's aid, then a decorative accessory. It must fit properly and be kept in
perfect repair. Most of our show tack is custom-made. Hermès and Devon
Gladstone saddles are popular, and many of our show bridles are made by
James B. Wiebe III of Bennett's Saddlery in Brookfield, Connecticut.

Over the years, there have been very few changes in styles of tack for
hunters and jumpers. Appropriate appointments follow strict adherence to
traditions begun on the hunt field and modified by ASHA requirements.
Any changes have been subtle.

Horse show rules dictate what tack is acceptable; after that the choice
is based on a rider's taste and horsemanship needs. Tack can artfully
conceal conformation problems as well as improve a horse's performance.

At our barn the care and cleaning of the bridles is the grooms' responsibility, and the saddles are the responsibility of the riders. However tack
and equipment are a horseman's props and are ultimately *his* responsibility. Even Olympic medalist Conrad Homfeld checks and adjusts his tack
before he mounts up in the in-gate. He undoes the girth and resets the
saddle on the horse's back in case it has slipped back, then retightens the
girth for position and safety. All good horsemen should do this. You
should also check the bit and bridle to make sure they are properly adjusted before you ride.

A wall of bridles and halters provides decorative profusion for our tack room. Each bridle bears the name of a Beacon Hill rider or horse. All tack is also stamped with a number, for identification and security. Center (see arrow) is the bridle of our first champion hunter, Dillon, stamped Sasso 1, for one of our first successful riders, Michael Sasso.

Hunter Tack

Schooling

Every rider should have a bridle especially for schooling. There are two reasons for this. One is obviously the need to protect expensive show tack from extensive wear in workouts. But the second is, perhaps, more important. Schooling tack should be kept simple, using, perhaps, a plain snaffle. This gives the rider the chance to elaborate if he needs more help or control from his tack when he gets to the show ring. Schooling tack should at first employ the most lenient aids and attachments, unless you are dealing expressly with a training difficulty. Also, a horse may become accustomed to his bit and develop what we call a "plain" or dull mouth, one reason why you might want to change bits occasionally.

The schooling bridle should be leather, with a half-round or plain flat noseband. The noseband should fall one inch below the cheekbone. The purpose of the noseband is to hold the mouth closed so that the horse cannot evade the bit. We commonly use a D-ring snaffle for schooling. The bit should produce two or three wrinkles in the corners of the mouth when properly adjusted.

We use laced or braided reins, not flat ones, and only a single rein, with a snaffle bit. We do not use a martingale on a horse except to show (if he needs it), for serious schooling (close to a show situation), or as a training aid on a young horse.

We sometimes use a breastplate, depending upon the conformation of the horse. Its main function is to keep the saddle from sliding back. For a schooling session a horse wears both a baby pad and a foam rubber pad under the saddle for extra protection from soreness. The same saddles are used for schooling and showing, but with different pads.

We don't paint the horses' hooves with dressing for every schooling session, but they always wear bell boots to protect the coronet band, and whatever other equipment each particular horse requires.

Show

Tack for the hunter ring must be elegantly traditional and must not be distracting, and should complement the conformation of the horse. The saddle pad should show evenly, framing the saddle. The reins should fall to mid shoulder. A score of details make your appointments a part of the total picture. Also, the tack should not be too restrictive, as the rider's main objective in the hunter ring is to demonstrate the horse's good manners and freedom of pace and movement, though you may use a variety of bits, such as the twisted-wire snaffle, the full-cheeked snaffle, the pelham, or a full double bridle.

The bridle must fit properly and securely. The fit of the bit, the length of the leather straps, and the snugness of the keepers (the small leather holders for the straps) are primary concerns. A properly adjusted bridle should, ideally, have the leather straps kept in the middle hole, with all three buckles parallel, forming a horizontal line from the horse's eye. Keepers tend to stretch out with use and should be changed often. On page 115, James Wiebe has shared with us his directions for measuring a bridle.

Fig. 8-2. Playing Games, wearing a custom bridle made to perfectly complement a fine hunter profile. All the buckles are parallel, forming a horizontal line from the horse's eye. The noseband falls one inch below the cheekbone. The bit is adjusted properly and polished. The reins are laced. The throatlatch flatters the refined head and jowl line.

Fig. 8-3. The end of the reins should fall to the mid-shoulder point when pulled taut.

TABLE 8.1

DIRECTIONS FOR MEASURING A BRIDLE

1. Bit to Bit--Starting 3 finger widths above the
                corner of the lip, measure over the
                poll and back down to the same point
                on the other side. Allow for bits
                of abnormal proportions.

2. Point to Point--Starting just behind the horse's
                eye, measure over the poll to
                the same point on the other
                side. This measurement is used
                to locate the cheek buckles and
                should be horizontally behind
                the eye.

3. Noseband--Starting 2-3 fingers below the cheek-
                bone, measure around the nose. If
                your horse wears his noseband higher
                or lower, measure him accordingly.

4. Nose Head--Starting 2-3 fingers below the cheek-
                bone, measure over the poll to the
                same point on the other side (if you
                measured the nose higher or lower,
                adjust this measurement accordingly).

5. Throat--Measure around the neck starting just
                behind the left ear following the path
                the throatlatch should take. Measure
                only as tightly as you wish it to fit.

6. Browband--Starting just below and 2 fingers to
                the rear of the right ear, measure
                across the front of the forehead to
                the same point on the left side.

Bridles should also be chosen according to a horse's conformation as well as his needs. There are, for example, several types of nosebands, which are chosen both for appearance and as an aid to the rider, as in the case of the dropped noseband (see Jumper Tack, on pages 117–118).

In the case of regular nosebands, if you have a horse with a long or wide head, a wide leather noseband will make it look shorter. Similarly, don't choose a rolled bridle if you have a big-headed horse. The throatlatch, if narrow, can flatter a refined horse; if wider, it can make a thick neck and jowl line look slimmer.

A show bridle may be a bit fancier than a schooling bridle, with subtly designed stitching on the browband and noseband. The look you are after is elegant, plain, and well fitting.

A standing martingale may be used at a show if a horse requires it to keep his head level. It must be loose enough to allow movement. It attaches to the girth, under the horse's belly, and to the noseband under the chin. If it fits properly, you should be able to place three fingers under the yoke at the crest of the neck and pull it up to two inches under the neck. Most martingales have a rubber stopper at the joining of the yoke-to-neck attachment, which should be cleaned and changed often.

Breastplates are also used for the show ring, and often have fancy stitching for detail.

Most of our students use a sixteen-and-one-half-inch seat saddle, with some exceptions based on rider size. All saddles are stamped on the inside for security reasons and have brass nameplates on the back of the seat. We prefer a flat saddle without knee rolls, but we do allow suede knee rolls for security. We change stirrup leathers often because the leather stretches. The ideal holes for stirrup leathers are the ninth to eleventh holes, as this puts less stress on the leather and is tidy, leaving no long flapping pieces. We do not recommend punching a lot of extra holes in the stirrup leathers, as it will weaken them, causing tearing and possible injury. We use plain

Fig. 8-4a (left). The martingale must be adjusted correctly. You should be able to place three fingers under the strap at the crest.

Fig. 8-4b (right). A standing martingale should pull up two inches under the neck. A martingale is used to keep the horse's head at a certain level, but it must allow freedom of movement.

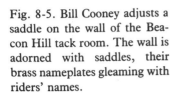

Fig. 8-5. Bill Cooney adjusts a saddle on the wall of the Beacon Hill tack room. The wall is adorned with saddles, their brass nameplates gleaming with riders' names.

leather girths unless a horse has a sore or a rub, in which case we use a fleece girth cover.

We also use washable fleece saddle pads to show. They should outline the saddle about one or two inches all around. Make sure you have enough pads—use at least two. If you need to use a foam pad, it is nice to cover it with washable imitation sheepskin for the show ring. We prefer the pads that attach to the billets of the saddle, but this is a matter of choice. It is imperative to keep saddle pads clean. They should be washed after every show.

Jumper Tack

Schooling

There is really very little basic difference between hunter and jumper schooling or show tack. Both should be as simple, properly fitted, and well cared for as possible. The only distinctions are the possible addition of dropped nosebands, the use of rubber reins, and the choice between running or standing martingales.

There are two types of dropped noseband used for schooling and in jumper classes: the converter, or flash, and the figure-eight noseband. The purpose of each is to keep the horse's mouth closed so that he cannot evade the bit. The converter is a separate piece of leather that attaches to the noseband in the center of the bridge of a horse's nose with buckles and extends down around the mouth. The figure-eight attaches to the cavesson, extending over the poll, then forms an X over the bridge of the nose, while the lower half of the figure-eight is fastened in front of the bit.

Jumpers are ridden with rubber-covered leather reins, with plain leather beginning at about the point of the shoulder. Rubber reins provide a better grip and won't stretch.

Baby pads and foam pads should be used under saddles in addition to fleece pads for cushioning to protect the horses' backs.

Show

Jumper schooling tack and jumper show tack are essentially the same. The only changes made for the show ring are those that depend upon the horse. You might use a different bit or ride in a running martingale.

A running martingale is attached to the girth in the same way as a standing martingale, but rather than being attached to the noseband, it splits into two parts at the yoke to form a Y. The reins thread through metal rings at the end of each strap. If the martingale fits properly, the rings should meet just in front of the withers when you pull them upward.

Breastplates are also used on jumpers to keep the saddle from slipping, depending on their conformation.

Spurs

Spurs are really a training aid, but, like tack, they should fit properly and be cleaned after using and/or before showing. For schooling and showing hunters and jumpers we prefer a half-inch blunt-tipped spur. This is an all-purpose spur and should fit the rider's boot halfway between the spur rest and the heel. The spur straps should be cut off so that they extend just beyond the keepers. Other spurs fit and are employed differently.

Fig. 8-6. Show jumper tack: Jenno Topping elected to use a figure-eight noseband and running martingale. Her horse, Reilly, also requires rundown bandages and splint boots.

Lead Ropes and Shanks

There are several types of lead shanks grooms and horseowners may use. Long-woven cotton lead ropes are used for bathing, shipping, and routine stable chores. Leather lead shanks with eighteen-inch chains that clip to the halter are used for leading a horse at shows, to lessons, or to schooling sessions. The lead can be clipped either to the ring of the bit or to the halter. These leather lead shanks cost upward of seventy dollars and are prized by grooms—many put their own names on them in brass. The chain, when laced through the noseband of the halter, provides better control of the horse when working with him or leading him. There is also a lead shank with a double chain and two clips that can be attached to both sides of the halter for longeing and other training situations.

Halters

You will need at least two halters for your horse: a nylon halter for bathing and a leather halter for grooming, trimming, and longeing (Figure 8.7). The leather halter can break under stress and is narrow enough to accommodate clippers. There are special shipping halters on the market, but we prefer leather halters covered with fleece to protect against abrasion.

Halters should fit correctly. The noseband should fall about an inch below the horse's cheekbone. Be sure the rings are not digging into his flesh or pinching him. You should be able to get two fingers under the strap at the chin and at the top of the poll to prevent rubs and allow the horse freedom to open his mouth. *We always remove halters when the horses are in their stalls or in the turnout paddocks.* This is important for the prevention of injuries. It is a good idea to become familiar with a horse's habits before you turn him out without a halter. He could be a problem to catch.

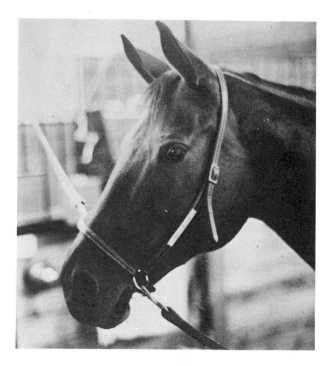

Fig. 8-7. A grooming halter, made of narrow leather, is used for most stable tasks, longeing, and shipping.

Fig. 8-8. Cleaning saddles is the responsibility of the riders at Beacon Hill. Here, three students find a corner in which to catch up on their chores.

Cleaning

Tack should be cleaned after every use. You have to remove sweat and grime and replace natural oils. Dirt and sweat are destroyers of tack. They eat away stitching and rot leather. And you have to be very careful to oil tack whenever it gets wet, as water evaporating on leather will draw out the natural oils.

The best time to clean a saddle and bridle is right after you ride. If you can't do this, set aside a time to go over your tack. Check for spots that need repair and leather that is stretching. We go over tack daily. Most riders will find tack and leather repair stores nearby. The very ambitious, or those with time enough, can repair their own with an awl and waxed thread.

One of the best substances for cleaning tack is glycerine soap. It comes in bar form, and to use it you simply wet it with a sponge and rub the surface of your tack with the lather. Then wipe the lather off with a towel. Be sure to unbuckle and remove straps from keepers and to clean crevices with a toothbrush. After cleaning your tack, replace lost oils with a conditioner/oil replacer such as Lexol. Always use an animal fat on leather, not a vegetable oil. Before you ride, passing a damp sponge once over the leather will release these oils, which will have penetrated the leather. The sponge will also blend in marks made by readjusting stirrup leathers or bridles.

Brass nameplates should be polished with brass cleaner; buckles, bits, and stirrup irons with a metal polish such as Duraglit. White rubber stirrup pads should be cleaned with a cleanser such as Comet, or ammonia. Fifteen minutes every time you ride is worth the hours of hard cleaning you will have to spend if you don't keep up with your tack.

Once a year, tack should be taken apart completely and stripped with ammonia and water for a thorough cleaning. Ammonia is devastating to the oil in leather, so don't use this cleaning method too often, and make sure you oil the tack with neat's-foot oil *immediately* after you strip it. When stripping tack, use a toothbrush to get into all the holes and buckle keepers, and use a razor to scrape off built-up oil and conditioners. Stitching is best cleaned with a mild soap such as Ivory.

Storage

If you know you will not be using your tack for a while, you should put it away in such a fashion that it will retain its moisture and keep you from having to clean it during the rest period. To do this, first take your bridle apart completely, and remove the girth and stirrup leathers from your saddle. Strip the parts, and clean them thoroughly. Then, apply a liberal coating of Vaseline and roll the separate pieces up in wax paper; store them in a trunk in a dry place. When you remove your tack, you will find it still supple and well oiled. This method also protects it from dry rot and mold.

Shipping

We provide custom-made trunks and saddlebags for our riders and recommend trunks for carrying equipment. We set them up in front of their horses' stalls in the barn or at a show. Away from home the trunks are the riders' lockers, where they store all the equipment needed for their horses and also their personal supplies. Inside you might find coolers, show pads, rain sheets, paddock boots, hairnets, crops, spurs, hats, and other rider/horse paraphernalia. Saddles and bridles are carried in water-resistant saddlebags, which protect the tack from scratches and dirt and keep everything together. Beacon Hill trunks carry all the other equipment, such as clippers, extension cords, hardware, medicines, tack cleaning implements, lead shanks, and halters, and the grooms travel with their own bandage and tack boxes. Everything bears the Beacon Hill logo and is in the Beacon Hill colors—navy, gray, and burgundy.

9

Grooming the Rider

What's so great about Bill and Frank is that they
find your hidden talents and develop them. They
take pride in presenting the individual rider within
the discipline of their regimes. Bill deals intellectu-
ally with the rider. Frank is concerned with body
position and control of the horse by the rider.

Beacon Hill student

We are constantly working on the total impression the horse and rider
make in the ring. The reality of the situation is that no matter how well
schooled or magnificent the horse is, it is the rider that most people notice
first. We want our riders to be as carefully turned out as our horses. There
is a look we aim for, one that is classic and tasteful, with meticulous
attention to detail. The rider must not stand apart from the horse, and we
do everything we can to make the two mesh together in an ideal picture
that we strive to produce.

Most of our clients have a marvelous sense of what looks right and an
appreciation of what we want. If they don't, they quickly learn what we
expect!

Rider Fitness

The first subject we tackle with a rider is his or her weight. It is
important that riders be as trim as possible. First of all, it makes them
agile and athletic. Second, it produces a much more pleasing picture. Most
of our young riders are careful about their diets. We hear stories about the
girls sneaking ice cream into their motel rooms, but they never let us see

them eating anything fattening at shows. They have to be serious enough about showing to lose weight if we think they should.

We also concentrate on rider fitness. If we see a rider who is winded after riding, we suggest that he or she take up a jogging or running program to build up endurance. A couple of years ago, Melanie Smith, a member of the 1984 Olympic show jumping team, took up running five miles a day to build up endurance.

After taking care of weight and overall fitness, we deal with specific trouble spots. After all, riders are athletes. They have to be strong and fit. If they have weak arms and can't hold their horses properly (for example, a strong horse in a jump-off, or a young horse that is pulling), we put them on a weight-lifting regime for their arms and back. If they have weak legs, thighs, or calves, we design a program of weight lifting and Nautilus therapy.

Dressing for Show

In terms of what we like to see in a rider's overall appearance, let's start from the head and work down. Even weekend riders should adhere to certain standards of dress—not just for looks, but for function and safety.

All our riders are required to wear hard hats at all times when riding—even for trail riding. Hair must be tucked up neatly under the cap in a hair net, even for lessons and warm-ups. This is simply a matter of forming good habits. We don't hesitate to tell a girl to fix her hair if stray ends are trailing.

We prefer black velvet riding hats with a long brim for safety and looks. The brim will actually protect your face, especially your nose, in a fall. A 1985 AHSA rule also requires that junior riders wear a heavy, buckled chin strap with a chin guard with their riding cap as a safety precaution. The strap should be cut so it extends just past the buckle.

A word about makeup and earrings. We like subtle, tasteful makeup—a natural look. Most of our riders are under eighteen, and many are thirteen to fifteen, so excessive makeup is obviously not necessary. Also, we insist upon small earrings, if they are going to wear them. Anything dangling below the earlobe could get caught in something when you ride. Small earrings are also less distracting and look more refined. We don't believe riders should wear any other jewelry—no stock pins, bracelets, or rings. Slim watches are acceptable. And our riders wear black leather gloves, never brown.

Though we are traditionalists, our attire for hunter and jumper classes does reflect some of the trends and fashions of the last decade.

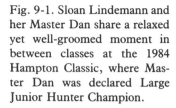

Fig. 9-1. Sloan Lindemann and her Master Dan share a relaxed yet well-groomed moment in between classes at the 1984 Hampton Classic, where Master Dan was declared Large Junior Hunter Champion.

Originally, the shadbelly was worn on the hunt field. Today, we sport the hunt coat. We prefer jackets made of worsted gabardine wool, in black, charcoal, navy, or a subtle pinstripe. Navy is a rider's best bet, because it is acceptable in most classes.

Jackets must be worn just long enough to reach the saddle. They take a lot of wear and tear, and should be cleaned often because otherwise they get frayed and lose their form. Brush them off with a slightly dampened towel and a clothes brush before a class. Buttons are always getting lost, and one of our riders has solved the problem by pinning, instead of sewing, her customized fox-head buttons onto her jacket. She simply unpins them when she sends it to the cleaners.

We suggest that our riders wear pale-colored shirts, or ones with a delicate stripe, with their jackets. Never wear a pinstriped jacket and striped shirt. If shirts have monograms, these should be small.

We prefer beige and rust britches. If you wear rust, don't wear the kind with white knee patches—they are too distracting and break up the line of the leg. Girls with heavy legs should wear rust. And nothing looks worse than the line of an undergarment showing through a pair of britches.

We are fanatical about belts being worn with britches. An open jacket exposing a beltless waistband looks awful on a course. A narrow belt with a small buckle is best.

Either field boots or dress boots are acceptable, whichever the rider prefers and is more flattering to the leg. Field boots hug the legs better and have laces across the instep to keep them lighter. The black dress boot has a more elegant line and no laces. A boot must fit exactly, coming to the bend in the rider's knee.

Boots are a safety precaution and also a functional riding aid. A rider—even a weekend rider—should always wear a boot with a heel, never a flat shoe. You can easily get hung up in the stirrup without a heel to protect you, and if you should get thrown, the heel prevents your foot from sliding all the way through the stirrup, which could catch your ankle and cause serious injury. If you can't get your foot out, you could get dragged or stepped on by the horse. Boots are also needed to strengthen leg aids and to hold spurs.

The care of boots is very important. They should be spit-and-polish clean and shiny, polished so that even the ridges and seams are clean. A toothbrush works wonders, and we recommend a cream boot polish. Our riders use Properts. Boots should always be dusted off before mounting and right before you go into a show ring.

As with the chin straps on hard hats, spur straps must be cut so that they extend just past the buckle. Flapping leather breaks the classic look of horse and rider. It is this kind of meticulous attention to detail that we feel separates a well turned out rider from the rest.

We carry this attention to detail right down to the numbers on a rider's back. We ask our riders to cut the corners off the big, square numbers handed out at horse shows, so that they are smaller, conform to the small of the back, and don't flap when our students ride (Figure 9.2).

Fig. 9-2. Jenno Topping, sporting an example of clipped corners on the numbers worn at horse shows.

Dressing for Schooling

For flat work, trail riding or lessons, we expect our students to be neatly attired in suede chaps without fringe, paddock boots, a hard hat, and gloves. They may wear clean jeans and a sweater or knit shirt if they wish.

Appointments and Accessories

When students come to Beacon Hill, we provide them with a wardrobe of necessary blankets—cooler, scrim, wool blanket, wool liner, rain sheet, and thermal blanket—all done in the Beacon Hill colors and insignia. The stable colors are navy with a narrow gray and burgundy border stripe, and letters in gray and white. These are kept in trunks that are also in the Beacon Hill colors. On a show day all the riders will be asked to use the same blanket, cooler, or scrim. The appearance of, say, ten horses in navy coolers at the in-gate can be an awesome sight to behold. This is show business, after all.

Riders also have their tack (if they have four or more horses, they should have at least two saddles for showing to avoid tacking problems during classes), crops—a short one for the hunters, a longer one for the jumpers—rain gear for themselves, and saddlebags for their saddles and bridles.

Riders should also be constantly aware of how their horses are turned out. They may have all the help they need from trainers and grooms, but they are the ones to whom it should matter most. It will make the difference in the ring. For hunters, packaging is everything, and the way the horse and rider look in the ring should remind a viewer of the hunt field— simple, functional, neat.

From our point of view, grooming the rider is a mental as well as a physical discipline. If the riders are prepared, showing becomes a matter of following routines, and this takes a lot of pressure off.

10

On the Circuit

If two horses tie for a class, I will make the horseman's decision and pin the one that looks the way a
horse should be turned out. I want my ribbon on a
horse that looks like a winner. Grooming is the
winning edge.

Randy Roy
AHSA judge

Let's face it, a class is won by performance. But when you have two or
three horses that have all done a superb job, it is very often the horse that
stands out a bit, presenting the classic hunt picture, that wins. We like
that phrase, "Grooming is the winning edge." Making a horse fit to show,
giving him that edge, is a lengthy process, one in which you can't make the
grade if you don't do your homework every day.

As we said at the outset of this book, what we try to do on the show
circuit is simply continue the day-to-day routines we follow for our horses
at home. Our grooms and staff go with us on the road. For shows like the
Hampton Classic in Bridgehampton, New York, the AHSA finals in Harrisburg, Pennsylvania, or those on the Florida winter circuit, we take our
entire barn with us—right down to the saddle racks and feather dusters.
The stalls are set up exactly like the ones at Beacon Hill to accommodate
our horses and riders in the same way.

We pride ourselves on a spotless, functional, and attractive show aisle
and have won some of the awards given at the top shows for the most
attractive tack stall. We set up an antechamber in front of the tack stall
with navy blue draperies, equestrian prints, mirrors on the walls, mahog-
any furniture, and gray carpeting. We plant fresh flowers in the wood
chips in the aisleway, and have a bouquet of flowers in the tack stall. In
many ways your tack stall is a public statement and the first impression
your stable makes at a show.

Fig. 10-1. Kristi Gertsner had The Artesian fit to show and was named Leading Junior Rider at the 1984 International Show Jumping Derby in Portsmouth, Rhode Island.

Fig. 10-2. The Beacon Hill tack room at the National Horse Show at Madison Square Garden in New York City, November 1984.

We also set up additional grooming stalls in all the aisleways to make it easy to work. Sometimes we have as many as three corridors of stalls. Our show barns are run exactly like our barn at home. Work sheets and assignments are posted every night—we take the same writing boards with us. The only difference is that we are at a show to do just one thing, to do our very best, whatever it takes.

Everything we do is geared to that end.

Come along with us on the show circuit and share a "realistic" day. Get some idea of how our daily routines come together in practice. Most of you are probably interested in showing, and this is where a routine either works or it doesn't. We've chosen to look back at a typical day at the Hampton Classic, one of the more prestigious shows on the East Coast, held annually at the end of August in Bridgehampton. It involves a full week of showing. At this particular show we had twenty-five horses with us and we took nine grooms. In addition, we had John Ducharme, Marion Hulick, Bernie LaRocque, and George Fitzgerald, who made a special trip to shoe six of the horses, and the two of us. The team was assembled.

The first thing we watch for at the Hampton Classic is the change in the nighttime weather. It starts to get chilly toward the end of August, and this is the show where we traditionally begin to use sheets, wool coolers, and blankets. Starting at midnight, Bernie LaRoque and his staff begin to braid twenty manes and tails for the day's classes.

At a hunter/jumper show, one horse and rider might go into three or four classes. Some riders have two or three horses; if you add it up, you will realize how hectic it can get for trainers and grooms. The ground is

Fig. 10-3. Our dear friend and consultant Marion Hulick shares an in-gate moment with us at the 1984 Hampton Classic.

Fig. 10-4 (left). All the horses' legs are washed with Ivory or a mild aloe-based soap before a class, or before they are put in support bandages for the night.

Fig. 10-5 (right). Show grooming essentials you will need to have on hand ringside to deal with any situation: hole punch * plastic container with caulks * wrenches to pull out caulks * hoof pick * hoof oil * Ace bandage for tail wrap * brushes * nearby—fly spray; in pocket—rub rag; in the rain—sheets and cooler

always cold and wet when the grooms begin to work at a horse show, even if it is the hottest day of the summer. They have to get the horses fed, groomed, possibly bathed, and tacked for their classes, some of which commence at around 8 A.M. Often, grooms will have all three of their horses in a single class.

First, they pick out their horses' feet, remove the cotton from the caulks, take off the bandages (if any), and wash off the legs. While the horses are eating, the grooms muck out the stalls. The horses are scheduled for flat work, a lesson, longeing, or hand walking. The trick is to get the horses ready without getting them excited.

Next, the grooms take off the horses' sheets and groom them as usual. Most of the horses' coats already look pretty clean and shiny; many have been bathed the night before, if not with soap, then with a Vetrolin body brace. Then, if a horse becomes sweaty again—remember, this is summer—he may be given a bath before his class, but we try to avoid this if his mane and tail have already been braided. He may be rinsed off instead.

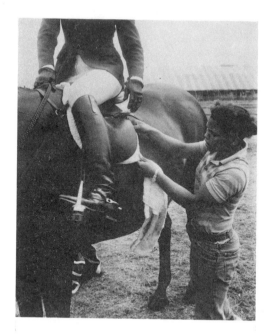

Fig. 10-6. It can't happen without an attentive groom. Even the most minute detail cannot be overlooked. Here Beth Furr tugs at a fleece pad to even the "frame" it makes for the saddle —part of the winning edge.

By 7 A.M., the aisleways are positively frenetic. Bernie is finishing up the last few manes and tails in the back grooming stall. Riders are shaking loose the cobwebs in their minds as they zip on their chaps for morning work. There is a constant parade of horses out to the schooling area. Grooms are walking horses wearing coolers in laps around the tents after their workouts. Now teamwork comes into play: A groom hands off one horse that is cool to another groom to tack while he rushes up to the schooling ring to bring back his second horse. Tack has been cleaned and adjusted, and all the pads and bandages laundered during the night in a local laundromat by a handful of grooms. Just before a class, saddles and bridles are rubbed clean with a damp towel.

Minutes before a class, everything comes to a peak. One rider is capturing her hair in a net, using one of the painted hunt mirrors we brought to decorate the front tack stall. Around the corner, another young woman is hastily polishing her spurs and irons. All of a sudden, it is discovered that there will not be enough time to bathe one of the horses. There are only twenty riders to go in the ring, about twenty-five minutes. As a groom tacks another horse he discovers that the martingale was incorrectly attached the night before and the buckle is facing backward. A team of three grooms deals with this crisis. A girl who has just walked in from the schooling area with her horse has been careful about keeping his legs white by staying on the grass. When the boots come off, the legs are spotless. "Thank you," says a happy groom. The horse that needs the bath is still being braided by Bernie, but he is rinsed off, cooled out, receives twenty-four perfectly aligned braids, and makes it to the ring in time for his class.

We have to watch the ground conditions carefully. The show is on grass, and morning dew and rain can make the focting slippery. Today, we send a groom running from the ring to tell the other grooms to put medium caulks in all the horses' shoes because there was rain during the night.

At the ring, there is also drama. Grooms with horses still showing have set themselves up along the fence with their tack boxes handy and their coolers folded up and hung along the rails. Sometimes a groom will have two or three horses in a ring at once, and sometimes in two different rings. Everyone helps at this point. Horses that are ready to go are still wearing their scrims to keep the flies off. The grooms keep them walking to relax them. Right before the class, the groom removes the scrim or cooler and gives the horse a final rub with the rag. Hoof oil is reapplied, and the rider's boots get a polish, too. The rider receives a word of encouragement from her groom. Grooms are a lot like the parents of gifted children. They really do root for their riders and bask in the glory of a win.

The final moments before a rider enters the ring reflect the secret of our horses' turnout. It is really adding the gloss to a perfectly groomed horse. The hooves get a final wipe and the coat a final rub, the nostrils are

Fig. 10-7. Last-minute magic: Here a groom extends a front leg to make sure the girth is not pinching. To grooms, last-minute preparations are just the finishing touches on a job that takes 365 days a year—making a horse fit to show.

cleaned, and a little Vaseline or baby oil is added around the eyes to make them appear alert and glistening. The tail wrap is removed, bell boots are checked (or removed, before a hunter class), and fly spray goes on just before the horse enters the ring. We give the horse and rider a final once-over, then our hearts and minds turn to one thing only—hoping our riders give the best performance they can.

As soon as a horse is finished for the day, his groom takes the braids out of his mane and tail and wets them down for the next day's braiding. He then takes the caulks out of the shoes and packs the holes with hoof packing or cotton. He will have cooled his horse out a bit in the walk back to the stalls, but after the mane and tail are out, he will cool him thoroughly by walking him in laps around the show tents.

Grooms have tricks to make every moment count. One groom removes a piece of equipment every time she completes one lap. By the end of, say, fifteen minutes, she has probably had a soft drink and completely untacked her horse. Meanwhile, she will have left three buckets of water out in the sun behind the stalls. Now, she will either bathe or body brace her horse, using *warm water*.

Winding down after the show repeats the morning's work. For the riders it involves a critique and assignments for the next day. They clean their saddles, go over their clothes, and put away their tack and appointments. The horses are bathed and bandaged, with a blue icing gel for soothing or plain alcohol for tightening tendons as a precaution. Manes are wetted down in anticipation of another nighttime braiding. Today there was a heavy wind, so sheets were put on the horses early, before feeding.

We have, as usual, hired Horse-Watch to check our horses every few hours during the night, so that in the morning we will have information about how the horses are feeling—our main concern when making them "fit to show." At the International Show Jumping Derby one year, we surprised one horse's groom when we came to the stalls in the morning by asking, "He didn't sleep well last night, did he?" How did we know? It had rained the night before, and rain on show tents makes a terrible racket for a horse to sleep through. That's what we mean when we say we are concerned about whether our horses are contented and happy. A good groom or horseman always senses the way his horse is feeling.

Sometimes we feel we are making our operation sound a little like Shangri-La, but we are driving ourselves toward an ideal and this includes the way we turn out our horses. Accidents, crises, mistakes, and nature conspire against us all. The best thing we can do is just that—do our best, and cope!

Afterword

Our system is by no means the only way to get a horse fit to show. It is a personal one that has developed over the years through trial and error, and because of the wonderful horsemen who have been our teachers, associates, and friends. Our reason for sharing our methods with you is the hope that you can put any or all of it to work for you.

There seems no better time than right now, after you have just finished reading the book and have some inkling of the enormous task of caring for a show horse, to express our admiration and appreciation to our friend and associate Marion Hulick. Her knowledge and generosity in sharing her expertise, and her standard of excellence in caring for horses, make Marion a consummate horsewoman.

We would also like to give credit to Poncho Lopez, a man who is considered by many to be the horseman's horseman. For years he has been a stable manager for some of the finest show barns in the United States, most recently for Katie Monahan. Poncho is the man many turn to on the horse show circuit for advice and help in handling problems. Thank you, Poncho.

Index

Entries in italic refer to illustrations.